Dave Barry's Only Travel Guide You'll Ever Need

ALSO BY DAVE BARRY

Dave Barry's Only Travel Guide You'll Ever Need

DAVE BARRY

FAWCETT COLUMBINE

NEW YORK

A Fawcett Columbine Book
Published by Ballantine Books

LIBRARY OF CONGRESS CATALOGING-
IN-PUBLICATION DATA
Barry, Dave.
[Only travel guide you'll ever need]
Dave Barry's only travel guide you'll ever need/Dave
Barry.—
1st ed.
        p.   cm.
ISBN 0-449-90651-5
1. Travel—Humor. 2. Travel agents—Humor. 3. Travel—
Handbooks, manuals, etc.—Humor. I. Title.
PN6231.T7B35 1991
818'.5402—dc20   91-70649
                                                                    CIP

Book design by Beth Tondreau Design
Illustrations by Patrick O'Brien
Manufactured in the United States of America
First Edition: October 1991
10 9 8 7 6 5 4 3 2 1

*This book is dedicated to
Wilbur and Orville Wright,
without whom air sickness
would still be just a dream.*

Contents

*Dave Barry's Only Travel Guide
You'll Ever Need*

Introduction

Mankind has always had a yen to travel. Millions of years ago, Mankind would be sitting around the cave, eating raw mastodon parts, and he'd say, "Marge, I have a yen to travel." And Marge would agree instantly, because she had frankly reached the point where if she saw one more mastodon part, she was going to scream. So off they'd go, these primitive tourists, exploring new territory, seeing new sights, encountering new cultures, and eventually having their skulls bashed into tiny fragments by the Big Rock Tribe.

But that has not stopped us. No, the human race is far too stupid to be deterred from tourism by a mere several million years of bad experiences, and today we're traveling in larger numbers than ever. We travel because, no matter how comfortable we are at home, there's a part of us that wants—that *needs*—to see new vistas, take new tours, obtain new traveler's checks, buy new souvenirs, order new entrees, introduce new bacteria into our intestinal tracts, learn new words for "transfusion," and have all the other travel adventures that make us want to French-kiss our doormats when we finally get home.

Of course, traveling is much easier today than it used to be. A hundred years ago, it could take you the better part of a year to get from New York to California; whereas today, because of equipment problems at O'Hare, you can't get there at all. Also, in the olden days a major drawback to traveling was the fact that much of the world was occupied by foreign countries, which had no concept whatsoever of how a country is supposed to operate. Many of them did not accept major credit cards. Sometimes the people would not understand plain English unless you spoke very loud. A few of these countries—it's hard to believe this was even legal—*did not have television in the hotel rooms.*

So as you can imagine, traveling was often a harsh and brutal experience. In one case, a group of innocent American tourists was taken on a tour bus through a country the members later described as "either France or Sweden" and subjected to three days of looking at old, dirty buildings in cities where it was *not possible to get a cheeseburger.* It reached the point where the U.S. government was considering having U.S. troops, with special military minibars strapped to their backs, parachute into these countries to set up emergency restaurants.

Fortunately, however, most of these countries eventually realized the marketing advantages of not being so foreign. Today you can go to almost any country in the world and barely realize that you've left Akron, Ohio, unless of course you are so stupid as to go outside the hotel. "Never go outside the hotel": this is one of the cardinal rules of travel. Another one is: "Never board a commercial aircraft if the pilot is wearing a tank top."

These are just two of the many vital nuggets of information you'll find throughout this book. Another good thing about this book is, it doesn't mince words. The problem with most so-called experts in the travel industry is that they are—no offense—lying scum. These people *want* you to travel. That's how they make *money*. That's why they're called "the travel industry." So naturally they're going to tell you whatever they think you want to hear.

> YOU: So, are there modern hotels in Latvia?
>
> TRAVEL AGENT: Oh, yes. Very modern. *Extremely* modern.
>
> YOU: Have you been there?
>
> TRAVEL AGENT: Not *technically*, no, but I have perused almost all the way through a brochure about it, and I can assure you that the modernity of Latvian hotels is pretty much of a legend. "As modern as a Latvian hotel" is an expression that we frequently bandy about, here in the travel industry.

And then, of course, when you get there, you discover that the hotel elevator is powered by oxen, and you have to share a communal bathroom with several Baltic republics, and the toilet paper could be used to deflect small-arms fire. But at that point there are no representatives of the travel industry within a thousand miles. You'll never find *them* in Latvia. They spend *their* vacations at the mall.

Most travel guidebooks are the same way. For one thing, most of these books are filled with information that was gathered during the Truman administration. The writers never have time to update the information, because they're too busy cranking out next year's edition (NEW! REVISED! HIGHLY INACCURATE!). Also, no matter what destination these books are talking about, they'll tell you it's wonderful: "Even the most demanding traveler is bound to feel a warm glow after only a few days in Chernobyl . . ."

This is not that kind of travel book. We call them as we see them. If we think a country is awful, we're going to say so, *even if we've never been to this country and know virtually nothing about it.* That's the kind of integrity we have. Right off the bat, for example, we're rejecting Paraguay as a destination. "Stay the hell out of Paraguay" is another one of the cardinal rules of travel, and we'll be giving you many, many more of these time-tested axioms as we think them up.

And what qualifies us as a travel expert? For one thing, we frequently refer to ourselves in the plural. For another thing, we have been traveling for many years, dating back to when we were a young boy in the early 1950s and our father used to drive our entire family from New York to Florida in a car that actually got smaller with every passing mile, so that by the time we got to Georgia the interior was the size of a standard mailbox, but not as comfortable, and the backseat hostility level between our sister and us routinely reached the point where any object placed between us would instantly burst into flame.

Yes, we have many fond travel memories. You are going to read about every damned one of them. Also, we may decide to make you look at the color slides we took of our trip to the Virgin Islands, featuring nearly two dozen shots of the airplane wing alone.

But mostly this book is intended to help you, the modern traveler, plan and carry out your business and vacation travel adventures with a minimum of unpleasantness and death. Throughout this effort, we will try to remember the famous thirteenth century tourist Marco Polo, who, having managed against all odds and with great effort to cross Persia, the plateau of the Pamir, the forbidden regions of Kashgar, Yarkand, and Khotan, and the Gobi Desert, finally arrived at the legendary Kublai Khan's palace at Shang-tu, where he uttered the words that have served as an inspiration for travelers ever since: "What do you mean, *you don't have my reservation?*"

Planning Your "Trip to Paradise," or Possibly Beirut

Planning is a very important part of travel. Just ask Amelia Earhart, the famous woman aviatrix[1] who in 1937 attempted to fly around the world in a twin-engine Lockheed and disappeared somewhere in the South Pacific and was never heard from again. This kind of thing can really put a damper on your vacation, yet it can easily be prevented if you do a little advance research by asking some basic travel questions, such as:

1. Will you be flying on a twin-engine Lockheed?
2. Will you ever be heard from again?
3. Will there be meal service?

[1] "Aviatrix" means "deceased person"

Oh, I realize that not everybody likes to plan every step of a vacation. Some people would rather just grab a backpack and a sleeping bag, stick out their thumbs and start hitchhiking down the highway, enjoying the fun and adventure of not knowing "what's around the bend." Most of these people are dead within hours. So planning is definitely the way to go.

Step One is to decide on a destination. The two most popular travel destinations are:

1. Domestic
2. Foreign

The major advantage of domestic travel is that, with a few exceptions such as Miami, most domestic locations are conveniently situated right here in the United States. This means that, on a domestic vacation, you are never far from the convenience of American culture in the form of malls, motels, Chicken McNuggets, Charmin Bathroom Tissue, car-window suction-cup Garfield dolls, lawyers, etc. Also, the United States contains an enormous amount of natural beauty, although I do not personally prefer Nature as a vacation destination, because of various factors such as the Dirt Factor, the Insect Factor, and, of course, the Snake Factor (see Chapter Eight, "Camping: Nature's Way of Promoting the Motel Industry").

The United States also contains some history, most of which is located in special humidity-controlled rooms in Washington, D.C., heavily guarded by armed civil servants. Or, if you prefer to get "off the beaten path," you can simply hop in the car and travel the highways and byways of this great land of ours, visiting its many proud little dirtbag towns:

Dweebmont, Ohio
"Styptic Pencil Capital of the World"

Often there will be local fairs and festivals where the kids can ride on the Whirl-'n'-Puke while Mom and Dad enjoy tasty local cuisine such as french fried potatoes, fried chicken, fried onion rings, fried dough, and fried frying oil fried with fried sugar.

Of course, if rides are what you're after, you'll definitely want to visit one of the major Themed Attractions, such as Six Flags over a Large Flat Region, or the world-famous Walt Disney World of Hot Irritable Popcorn-Bloated Families Waiting in Enormous Lines (see Chapter Four, "Disney World on $263,508 a Day"). Many of these attractions feature exhibits simulating foreign nations such as Europe, thus enabling you to experience exactly what it would be like to be in another country, provided that it was a foreign country staffed by Americans and located inside a Themed Attraction.

But if you prefer the "real thing," you'll want to choose a foreign travel destination. The major problem here, as I mentioned in the Introduction, is that foreign destinations tend to contain enormous quantities of foreigners.[2] There's nothing you can do about this except grin and bear it, unless you're in some foreign country where grinning is considered rude and is punishable by death, in which case you should

[2] In the form of Japanese tourists

frown and bear it, or stick a finger up each nostril and bear it, or whatever they do when they bear it in that country.

But that's exactly the problem. As an American who was raised in America and attended American schools—where, despite years of instruction, the only thing you learned how to say in a foreign language is "The dog has eaten my brother"—you will often find yourself totally disoriented in foreign situations. Europe, for example, is filled with knots of confused Americans, squinting at menus with no more comprehension than a sea gull examining the Space Shuttle ("What the hell does *this* mean?" "I think it means 'Chicken of the Hot Trouser Parts.' ").

Also, you will have to accept the fact that, in foreign countries, you will never have the vaguest idea how much anything costs. All foreign countries have confusing money, with names like the Pound, the Yen, the Libra, the Mark, the Frank, the Duane, the Doubloon, and the Kilometer, all of which appear to have been designed by preschool children. Not one of these monetary units is equal to a dollar, or anything else, and all of them change in value on an hourly basis. This is all a result of the Marshall Plan, which was set up by General Marshall Plan after World War II as a means of making the entire rest of the world rich at our expense, the idea being that Americans traveling abroad would be so disoriented by foreign currency that every now and then one of them will buy a single croissant and leave a tip large enough to enable the waiter to retire for life.

But that's the fun of traveling abroad: the sense of

romance and mystery that comes from being an out-of-it bozo, from not knowing for sure whether the sign you're looking at says PUBLIC PARK or RADIOACTIVE WASTE AREA. One time I was with a group of five people driving around Germany, and it took us an *entire week* to figure out that "Einbahnstrasse" meant "One-Way Street." We'd be driving around some German city, frowning at our map, scratching our pointy American heads and saying, "Geez! We're on *Einbahnstrasse* again!" Ha ha! What a bunch of gooberheads we were! Fortunately, everybody in Germany, including domestic animals, speaks English better than the average U.S. high school graduate, so we were able to get clear directions from passing pedestrians. At times like these, you might tend to feel culturally inferior, as an American, but it's always heartening to remember that, no matter what country you're in, it probably doesn't rank anywhere *near* the U.S.A. in the nuclear-warhead department.[3]

PLANNING YOUR TRAVEL BUDGET

The standard formula for computing travel costs is to figure out the total amount of available money you have, total, then multiply this by at least six. But even this formula is probably going to give you a low estimate, because you usually have unexpected

---

[3] Also we have Wayne Newton

costs, as we can see by this Breakdown of Average Travel Costs:

Travel, lodging, food, tips—12%

T-shirts that you buy after four frozen drinks but that you can never actually wear because they say things like I GOT THE CRABS AT BIG DICK'S—17%

Incidentals—71%

What I mean by "incidentals" are those unexpected expenses that inevitably come up when you travel, such as buying replacement teeth, posting bail, bribing nuns, etc. My wife actually did bribe a nun once. We were in Rome, trying to get into a famous cathedral, which according to the guidebook contained large quantities of architecture and, more important, a bathroom (see map, page 15, "The Toilets of Europe"). Our guidebook said that the cathedral would be open, but when we got there our path was blocked by a large unforeseen nun, who told us by means of stern gestures that it was closed, even though we could see tourists walking around in there. Being a seasoned international traveler with a certain amount of "savoir-faire,"[4] I eventually realized what the deal was, so I slipped the nun a specific amount of Italian currency worth approximately 325,000,000,000,000 libras, which at the then-current rate of exchange was equal to roughly 57 cents American. Or it could have been several thousand dollars. There was really no way to tell. But I

[4] French, meaning "bladder discomfort"

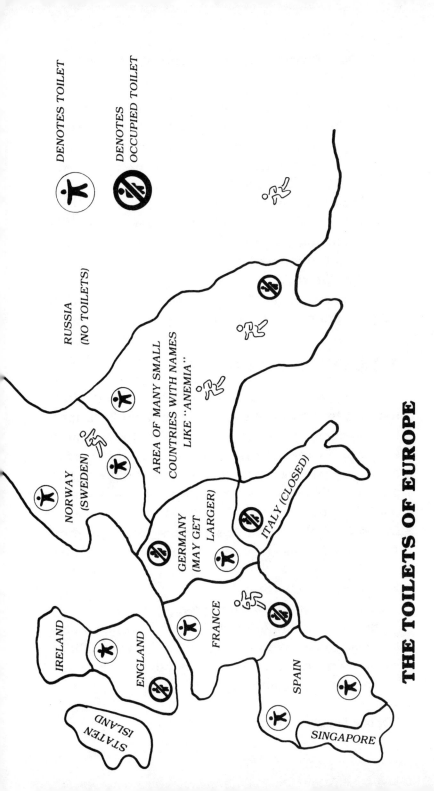

THE TOILETS OF EUROPE

do want to stress that, whatever amount it was, I am certain the nun turned it directly over to the church.[5]

My point is that whenever and wherever you travel, you're going to have unanticipated expenses, and you need to anticipate them. Fortunately the Visa and MasterCard people have a fine program for travelers, under which you can charge everything, and then when you get back, you simply pay them small convenient amounts for several years, which turns out to be nowhere near enough, so they confiscate your children, which is not entirely a bad thing (see Chapter Four, "Traveling as a Family").

TRAVELER'S CHECKS

Travelers checks are very impressive pieces of paper that are backed by the full faith and credit of actor Karl Malden. They are accepted at thousands of shopping locations around the world, although almost never the location that you personally are shopping in. Nevertheless, traveler's checks are very popular with those travelers who have the brains of frozen vegetables. You've seen these people in those American Express traveler's check commercials:

> FIRST TRAVELER: Oh no!
> SECOND TRAVELER: What's wrong!
> FIRST TRAVELER: I left my wallet unguarded on a café table here in the middle of this squalid, poverty-ridden, crime-infested foreign city, and now it's *gone*!

[5] Or she bought a Ferrari

SECOND TRAVELER: But that's impossible!

KARL MALDEN *(to camera)*: Hi, I'm Karl Malden.

FIRST TRAVELER: Look! It's Raymond Burr!

KARL MALDEN: If you lose your American Express traveler's checks, you can call for an immediate refund.

FIRST TRAVELER: But we don't even know how to operate a telephone!

SECOND TRAVELER: I don't even remember which Traveler I am! I think I'm the Second Traveler!

FIRST TRAVELER: No! *I'm* the Second Traveler!

KARL MALDEN *(to camera)*: American Express traveler's checks. A lot of people never even figure out how to cash them.

WORKING WITH A TRAVEL AGENT

You should definitely have a travel agent. Why go through all the hassle of dealing with airlines, hotels, and rental-car agencies yourself, only to see the arrangements get all screwed up, when with just a single phone call you can have a trained professional screw them up for you?

No, seriously, travel agents are wonderful. At least mine is. Her name is Ramona, and I'd literally be lost without her. I'll be on a business trip, and I'll wake up in a strange hotel room in bed with traces of minibar cheese[6] in my hair, and in a disoriented panic I'll call Ramona, and we'll have the following conversation:

[6] At $127.50 per ounce

ME: Where am I?

RAMONA *(checking her computer)*: You're in Houston.

ME *(alarmed)*: Why?

RAMONA: You're on a business trip.

ME: Can I come home yet?

RAMONA *(checking her computer)*: No. You have to go to Detroit.

ME *(very alarmed)*: Detroit?

RAMONA *(checking her computer)*: And get that cheese out of your hair.

I always do what Ramona says, because she has the computer. Ramona could ship me off to the Falkland Islands if she felt like it.

Ramona also is good at attempting to explain the airline fare system, which is governed by a powerful, state-of-the-art computer that somebody apparently spilled a pitcher of Hawaiian Punch into the brain of, and it has been insane ever since. I base this statement on the fact that if I fly from Miami to, for example, Tampa, the round-trip fare is often hundreds of dollars more than what it costs to fly from Miami to, say, Singapore. This makes no sense. Singapore is in a completely different *continent*,[7] whereas Tampa is so close to Miami that our stray bullets frequently land there. And what is worse, there is never just *one* fare to Tampa. There are *dozens* of them, and they are constantly mutating, and the more Ra-

[7] Possibly Africa

mona explains them to me, the more disoriented I become.

ME: I need to go to Tampa on Thursday.

RAMONA *(checking her computer)*: No, not Thursday.

ME: No?

RAMONA: No, because there's a $600 penalty if you fly on a Thursday during a month whose name contains two or more vowels following two straight quarters of increased unemployment *unless* you are a joint taxpayer filing singly with two or more men on base *provided* that you spend at least one Saturday night in a hotel room within twelve feet of a malfunctioning ice machine *and* you undergo a ritual initiation ceremony wherein airline ticket agents dance around you and put honey-roasted peanuts up your nose.

ME: Book me on the Singapore flight.

RENTING A CAR

Renting a car offers many attractive advantages to the traveler: independence, convenience, dependability, and a sudden, massive lowering of the IQ. I know what I'm talking about here. I live in Miami, and every winter we have a huge infestation of rental-car drivers, who come down here seeking warm weather and the opportunity to make sudden left turns without signaling across six lanes of traffic into convenience stores.[8] My wife and I have affectionately nicknamed these people "Alamos," because so many of them seem to rent their cars from Alamo, which evidently requires that every driver leave several major brain lobes as a deposit. We'll be driving along, and the driver in front of us will engage in some maneuver that is boneheaded even by the standards of Miami (official motoring motto: "Death Before Yielding"), and we'll shout, "Look out! Alamos!" We're tempted to stay off the highways altogether during tourist season, just stockpile food and spend the entire winter huddled in our bedrooms, but we're not sure we'd be safe *there*.

Not that I feel superior to the Alamos. I've rented many cars myself, and I have to admit that as soon as I get behind the wheel, I go into Bozo Mode. For one thing, I am instantly lost, and the only guidance I have is the rental-car-agency map, the sole function of which apparently is to show you the location of the rental-car agency. So I'm disoriented, plus I'm constantly trying to adjust the mirrors, seat, air conditioning, steering wheel, etc., plus—this is the most important part—I have to find a good radio station. This means I am devoting only about 2 percent of my brain to actually driving the car. And thus I—a person who tends to be *extremely* critical of other people's driving—am transformed into an Alamo, drifting along at 27 miles per hour in the left lane of the interstate, with my left blinker on, trying to locate the FM button. Maybe, as a warning to other drivers, the federal government should require that

[8] No, not into the parking lots. Into the *stores*

all rental cars must have giant orange question marks sticking up out of their roofs.

CHOOSING A CAR-RENTAL COMPANY

The car-rental industry is extremely competitive, and often you can find some really good "deals" by keeping your eyes "peeled" for advertisements that look like this:

Why Pay More?
Rent a Car for Just $3.99 a Week!!
Including *Unlimited Mileage!!*

Big Bob's Car Rental & Miniature Golf &
Full-Body Massage

Certain restrictions apply to this offer, such as to get the actual car you have to ride our "Courtesy Van," which runs only during Lent, from the airport to our rental facility, which is in the Soviet Union, where you will have to wait in line behind people who have been there since the Ford administration because our rental fleet consists of a 1971 Plymouth Valiant with a tendency to catch fire, so we *definitely* recommend the insurance.

As a "smart shopper," you will definitely save "big money" by taking advantage of bargains such as these, although you should of course insist that the agency person explain the terms of the rental agreement before you sign it:

YOU: What does this mean?

AGENCY PERSON: What does what mean?

YOU: This part here, where it says, "Renter agrees that we get to keep his house."

AGENCY PERSON: Oh, *that.* Nothing.

YOU *(relieved):* Whew.

TYPES OF LUGGAGE

The type of luggage you carry says a lot about you. For example, if you're carrying somebody *else's* luggage, it says you're a thief.

No, seriously, luggage is important, which is why most frequent travelers spend their entire lives looking for Exactly the Right Piece of Luggage, the one that is nice and compact but holds a lot of stuff. This is a waste of time, of course, because the truth is that a piece of luggage is nothing but a bag or a box with a handle on it, and under the laws of physics, which are strictly enforced in luggage, the size of the bag or the box determines how much it will hold, as can be seen in the following chart:

SIZE OF LUGGAGE UNIT	AMOUNT OF STUFF LUGGAGE UNIT WILL HOLD
Small	Small amount
Medium	Medium amount
Large	Large amount[9]

[9] But still not enough

The infrequent traveler generally accepts these limitations and purchases one of those enormous, hard-sided suitcases that have wheels and weigh about 87 pounds even when they're empty. But your frequent traveler never abandons the quest to find a miracle luggage unit that can hold more than it can actually hold. Over the course of a lifetime the frequent traveler will purchase dozens of luggage units, frequently from advertisements in airline in-flight magazines. You've probably seen the advertisements. There's a picture of what appears to be an ordinary carry-on suitcase, underneath which are about 70,000 words, which begin:

AMAZING LUGGAGE BREAKTHROUGH!

A recent scientific discovery by researchers at the Stanford University School of Luggage Science has made possible the REVOLUTIONARY new Laser 3000X Total Carry-on Wardrobe Unit! Although smaller than a standard clarinet case, this incredible unit, thanks to advanced luggage technology, can easily hold:
- Eight men's suits OR
- 14 women's full-length evening gowns PLUS
- All the shirts, socks, ties, underwear, and clothing accessories you would need for two terms in Congress PLUS
- All your toiletries PLUS
- *An actual working toilet*

And that's not all! How many times have you said to yourself, as a busy business traveler: "Why can't they design a carry-on bag with a space for my tennis rackets, golf clubs, skis, and volleyball equipment?" Well, look no farther, because the Laser 3000X . . .

And so on. Ordinarily you would take one look at this kind of advertisement and say, hey, get *serious*. But in the airplane environment, where you have nothing else to do except watch the movie,[10] you find yourself reading all the way through it, and by the time you're on your third Bloody Mary, and you've reached the part where the advertisement claims that this suitcase will do your tax returns for you, you're thinking, "Hey! This could be the answer to my luggage needs!" So you whip out your Visa or MasterCard and fill out the order form, and six to ten weeks later you receive: a bag with a handle. A *small* bag with a handle. Which, if you really pack it right, will hold two pairs of socks PLUS your dental floss. I know what I'm talking about! I have seventeen of these things!

HOW MUCH LUGGAGE YOU CAN CARRY ON A COMMERCIAL AIRLINE FLIGHT

Federal Airline Administration regulations state that each passenger may have up to 17,000 pounds of carry-on luggage *provided that he or she can jam it all into the overhead baggage compartment.* I am a veteran traveler, but I am still amazed at how much

---

[10] *Rocky XVII*, the one where he has surgery so his eyelids can open all the way

stuff some people will try to get up there. Entire households, sometimes. These people are always directly in front of me.

"What do you mean, I can't carry this on?!" they'll say to the airline personnel. "I ALWAYS carry this on!"

"Sir," the airline personnel will say, "that's a *lawn tractor*."

"But look!" the person will say. "It fits in the overhead baggage compartment!"

And the person will actually attempt to shove it in there, which is of course impossible because (a) the tractor is too large, and (b) the compartment already contains some other passenger's upright piano. But this will not stop the person from trying. No human emotion is more powerful than the grim determination of an airline passenger attempting to shove an inappropriate object into the overhead baggage compartment.

WHAT TO PACK

There are two major schools of thought on how to pack for traveling. These are known technically as "my school" and "my wife's school."

My school of packing is that you should never carry more things than you can fit into a standard sandwich bag. This way you never put yourself in a position where you have to turn your belongings over to a commercial airline's crack Luggage Hiding Department (traces of airline luggage have been found on Mars). So I travel very light, and I've found that this is really not a problem, once I get adjusted to the stench resulting from wearing the same shirts and socks and, of course, underwear for as long as two weeks running. The advantage of this is that I get plenty of room to stretch out on airplanes, because nobody will sit near me. The disadvantage is that the flight attendants also stay away, preferring to serve my dinner entree by flipping it at me Frisbee-style from as far as 25 feet away, and some of those airline entrees[11] are hard enough to kill a person.

My wife, on the other hand, would not think of leaving the house for even a half hour without sufficient possessions in her purse alone to establish a comfortable wilderness homestead. So when we travel, she packs many, many items. She buys these giant suitcases, manufactured by shipbuilders, and she packs them with items for every conceivable contingency. Like, if we're going someplace in the tropics, she'll naturally pack an entire set of lightweight outfits, but she'll also pack an entire set of *medium*-weight outfits, in case we have a cool snap; and a set of *heavy* outfits, in case we get locked inside a meat freezer; and a *waffle iron*, in case we get hungry for waffles while we're in there; and so on. So we generally arrive at the airport with virtually all of our worldly possessions, looking like Cambodian refugees, except that we appear to be actually taking Cambodia with us. Our carry-on luggage alone is enough to prevent many planes from ever leaving the ground. They'll taxi down the runway, gaining speed, then, after a violent grunting effort to take off,

[11] Such as lasagna

they'll continue right on taxiing, sometimes right into a harbor. This doesn't worry us, however, because my wife always brings plenty of scuba equipment.

BONUS PACKING TIP:
How to Pack a Suit So It Won't Come Out Wrinkled

Lay the suit on its back on a flat surface such as a tennis court. Take the sleeves and place them at the side. Take the *left* sleeve and place it on the suit's hip, and hold the *right* sleeve over the suit's head as though the suit is waving in a jaunty manner. Now put *both* sleeves straight up over the suit's head and shout, "Touchdown!" Ha ha! Isn't this fun? You may feel stupid, but trust me, you're not *half* as stupid as the people who think they can fold a suit so it won't come out wrinkled.

How to Speak a Foreign Language in Just 30 Minutes

WITHOUT NECESSARILY HAVING ANY IDEA WHAT YOU ARE SAYING

One of the great things about being an American, aside from the constitutionally guaranteed freedom to have obscene bumper stickers, is that so many foreign people speak our language.[1] You can walk the streets of just about any major city in the world, and as soon as the natives realize that you're an American, they'll make you feel right at home.

"Stick them up!" they'll say. "Please to be handing over your American Express traveler's checks! Don't leave home without them!"

Yes, they are clever, those natives. Nevertheless, you may sometimes find yourself in a foreign situa-

---

[1] English

tion wherein members of the local population, because of a poor educational system or sheer laziness, have not learned to speak your language fluently. This can lead to serious problems, as when for example you're in Spain, attempting to obtain a chicken-salad sandwich, and you wind up with a dish whose name, when you look it up in your Spanish-English dictionary, turns out to mean "Eel with the Big Abscess." This is why I strongly recommend that before you travel abroad, you learn to speak a foreign language, ideally the same one that is spoken in whatever country you're going to.

Of course you probably think it's hard to learn another language, because you spent years studying foreign languages in high school, and all you can remember is being forced to confiscate verbs and memorize those moronic dialogues wherein everybody seemed to be obsessed with furniture:

PIERRE: Voici le bureau de mon oncle. ("Here is the bureau of my uncle.")

JACQUES: Le bureau de votre oncle est right prochain de la table de ma tante. ("The bureau of your uncle is right next to the table of my aunt.")

MARIE: Qui donne un merde? ("Who gives a shit?")

I took an estimated two thousand years of high school French, and when I finally got to France, I discovered that I didn't know one single phrase that was actually useful in a real-life French situation. I could say, "Show me the fish of your brother Raoul," but I could *not* say, "Madame, if you poke me one more time with that umbrella I am going to jam it right up one of your primary nasal passages," which would have been extremely useful.

So what you need, as a traveler, is to learn *practical* foreign expressions. Let's say you're in a very swanky Paris restaurant that has earned the coveted "Five-Booger" ranking from the prestigious *Michelin Guide to How Snotty a Restaurant Is*. You cannot be asking these people to show you the fish of their brother Raoul. You will want to use simple, foolproof phrases such as the following.

PRACTICAL FRENCH RESTAURANT PHRASES

—Garçon! Je suis capable de manger un cheval! ("Waiter! I could eat a horse!")

—Apportez-moi quelques aliments française ici pronto sur la double! ("Bring me some French food immediately!")

—Mettez-le smaque dabbe sur la table. ("Put it smack dab on the table.")

—Attendez une minute au jus dernier! ("Wait just a darned minute!")

—Qu'est-ce l'enfer que c'est? ("What is this the hell that this is?")

—Attemptez-vous à yanquer ma chaine, boudet? ("Are you trying to yank my chain, buddy?")

—Je donne madam CHAT plus viande que cette! ("I give my damn CAT more meat than this!")

—Sacre moo! Ce EST mon chat! ("Holy cow! This IS my cat!")

OTHER PRACTICAL FRENCH PHRASES

—Nous sommes suppose a faire peepee ICI? ("We're supposed to pee HERE?")

—Mais nous sommes droit dans le friggant RUE. ("But we're right in the goshdarn STREET.")

—Il y a des RELIGIEUSES regardant nous. ("There are NUNS watching us.")

—Dites, cette religieuse est hot. ("Say, that nun is fairly attractive.")

—Peut-etre j'ai been en France trop longue. ("Perhaps I have been in France too long.")

PRACTICAL SPANISH PHRASES
In the Restaurant:

—Camarero, hay una mosca en mi sopa. ("Waiter, there is a fly in my soup.")

—Pero esa mosca es atarado al *pantalones*. ("But this fly is attached to a pair of *pants*.")

Riding Public Transportation:

—¿Jey, no es anybody *pilotando* ese autobus? ("Hey, isn't anybody *driving* this bus?")

—¿ESE es el piloto? ("THAT'S the driver?")

—¿El hombre que dormir en el charco de saliva? ("The man sleeping in the puddle of saliva?")

—Quiza deberias empujar los frenos. ("Maybe we should apply the brakes.")

—¿Que the hell usted decir, una cabra ha comido

los frenos? ("What do you mean, a goat ate the brakes?")

—¿Porque estan mi frente marcas de preguntas al reves? ("Why are my front question marks upside down?")

During Festivals:

—Mi (esposo, esposa) es been tramplado por toros. ("My [husband, wife] has been trampled by bulls.")

—No, no estoy quejarsando. ("No, I'm not complaining.")

Emergency Medical Phrases:

—¡Muchacho, es mi booty dolorido desde ese caso de los trots! ("Boy, is my butt sore from this diarrhea!")

—¡El hace yo pasar como el tarde Campos de Totie! ("It's making me walk like the late Totie Fields!")

PRACTICAL ITALIAN PHRASES

—Non desear chiunque ferire or nothing. ("We don't want anybody should get hurt.")

—Tuo fratello Raoul dormi con los pesces. ("Your brother Raoul sleeps with the fishes.")

PRACTICAL GERMAN PHRASES

—Achtung! ("Gesundheit!")

—Enschreitenblatten Schalteniedlich Verkehrsge-
sellschaft! ("Ha ha!")

—Ich veranlassenarbeitenworken mein Mojo. ("I
have got my mojo working.")

Air Travel

(OR: WHY BIRDS NEVER LOOK TRULY RELAXED)

You're probably not going to believe this, but there are still some people, in this modern day and age, who are afraid of air travel. Ha ha! Are they a bunch of Nervous Nellies, or *what*?

Oh, sure, air travel *seems* dangerous to the ignorant layperson, inasmuch as it involves hurtling through the air seven miles straight up trapped inside an object the size of a suburban ranch home in total defiance of all known laws of physics. But statistics show that, when you're in an airplane, you're actually *four times as safe* as when you're driving your car on an interstate highway![1]

[1]Provided that you are driving drunk and blindfolded

Nevertheless, many of us, even veteran fliers, tend to be a little edgy about air travel these days, because it seems as if hardly a day goes by that we don't pick up a newspaper and see headlines like:

ENGINE FALLS OFF PLANE

WING FALLS OFF PLANE

PILOT SUCKED OUT OF PLANE

PLANE POSSESSED BY DEMONS
FAA Orders Exorcism of Entire L-1011 Fleet

But the truth is that, thanks to improvements in technology, air travel today is safer than it has been at any time for the past three weeks. Yes, we've come a long way since the Age of Aviation began back in the historic year of 19-something in Kitty Hawk, North or South Carolina, when two young mechanics named Wilbur and Orville Wright, using some canvas and old bicycle parts, constructed the very first airline omelet. There have been many important commercial-aviation innovations since then, including:

- *Airline magazines* featuring articles with titles like "Akron: Meeting Yesterday's Challenges Tomorrow."
- *"Turbulence."* This is what pilots announce that you have encountered when your plane strikes an object in midair. You'll be flying along, and there will be an enormous, shuddering WHUMP, and clearly the plane has

HOW AN AIRPLANE FLIES

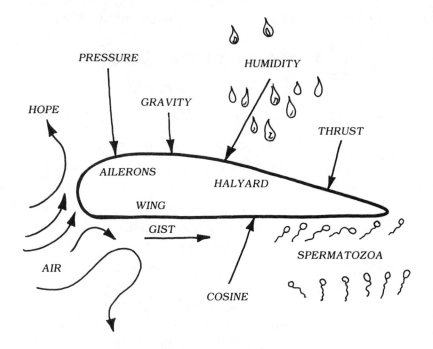

As the engine increases the thrust, pressure and humidity start to increase, causing the plane to taxi down the runway, which in turn produces a buildup of concern in the cockpit until the plane is going 150 miles per hour and headed directly for the interstate, whereupon the pilot and co-pilot grip the controls with all their strength and go "NOOOOOOOOOOOOOOOOOO!!!!!" whereupon the entire plane lunges into the air and quite frankly it beats the shit out of us how come it does.

rammed into an airborne object at least the size of a water buffalo, and the pilot will say, "Folks, we're encountering a little turbulence." Meanwhile they are up there in the cockpit trying desperately to clean water-buffalo organs off the windshield.

- *Frequent-flier programs*, wherein each time you take a commercial flight, you earn a certain number of miles, plus bonus miles if you actually reach your intended destination within your lifetime. After you've accumulated enough miles, you can redeem them for *another* flight, unless you have the intelligence of a turnip, in which case you'll remain in your recreation room, where it's safe.

- *The Baggage Carousel*, where passengers traditionally gather at the end of a flight to spend several relaxing hours watching the arrival of luggage from some *other* flight, which comes randomly spurting out of a mysterious troll-infested tunnel that is apparently connected to another airport, possibly in a different dimension.

- *The baby in the seat behind you* whose parents are obviously poking it with hat pins because there is no other way that a child could shriek that loudly all the way from New York to Los Angeles.

- *The 475-pound man in the adjacent seat* who smells like a municipal landfill and whose forearm (which by itself is the size of Roseanne Barr) spends the entire flight oozing, like the Blob, over the armrest until it occupies virtually your entire seat and starts absorbing your in-flight meal through some of its larger pores. This in itself is not a bad thing, because airline food is not intended for human consumption. It's intended as a form of in-flight entertainment, wherein the object is to guess what it is, starting with broad categories such as "mineral" and "linoleum." When the flight attendants ask, "Do you want roast beef or lasagna?" they don't mean, "Do you want roast beef, or do you want lasagna?" They mean: "Do you want this dinner substance, which could be roast beef, or it could be lasagna? Or possibly peat moss?"

And speaking of airline food, another important aviation development has been:

• *The barf bag.* Early barf bags were large canvas sacks; a severely airsick passenger would be placed inside, and the bag would then be sealed up and, in an act of aviation mercy, shoved out the cargo door at 12,000 feet. Today's passenger doesn't get that kind of personalized service, and must place a small bag over his nose and mouth in hopes of cutting off his oxygen supply.

Despite these strides forward, there have been a few problems caused by the belt-tightening in the airline industry that has resulted from "deregulation," a new government policy under which the only requirement to purchase an airline is that you have to produce two forms of identification. Even Donald Trump was allowed to purchase an airline, which he immediately named after himself ("Air Jerk"). This led to some dramatic aviation moments when Trump got into financial difficulty and had to sell some of his aircraft *while they were still in the air*. ("This is your captain speaking. We've just been advised that instead of Boston, we will be landing in Iran. We regret any incon . . .")

Of course, this kind of adventure only adds to the fun of flying. My family has had many fun flights, including an extremely exciting one in which we went from Miami to Honolulu via the following itinerary, which I am not making up:

1. We flew from Miami to Denver on a plane that seemed to be working fine, so naturally they made us get off of it and get on *another* plane that was supposed to fly the rest of the way to Honolulu. This happened to be on Halloween. "Never Fly on Halloween," that is our new aviation motto.

2. They put a bunch of fuel on our new plane, and we got on it. One of the flight attendants was wearing devil ears, which struck us as hilarious at the time but which we later on realized was an omen. "Never Get on a Flight Where a Crew Member Is Wearing Devil Ears" is another one of our aviation mottoes.

3. When we got out to the end of the runway, the pilot announced that we had *too much* fuel, which struck us ignorant laypersons as odd, because we were under the impression that having a lot of fuel is *good*, especially when you're flying over a major ocean such as the Pacific. Nevertheless we went back to the gate and got off the plane while they removed fuel, apparently using eyedroppers, because it took them two hours.

4. We got back on the plane and the pilot announced that—remember, I am not making this up—we were going to fly to Los Angeles to get some *more* fuel. So needless to say . . .

5. We landed in San Francisco. There they told us (why not?) that we had to change planes, so we all got off, only to be met by a gate attendant wearing *an entire devil costume*, which was seeming less and less amusing. Also the pilot was not inspiring a great deal of confidence in us. You know how pilots are generally trim, military-looking individuals who remain up in the cockpit looking aloof but competent? Well, *our* pilot was a chunky, slightly disheveled man who looked like a minor character in *Police Academy XIII*. He was walking around the lounge area, chatting with us passengers as though he had nothing else to do, and holding a computer printout the thickness of *War and Peace*, which he announced was our "flight plan," although we couldn't help but note that (a) he wasn't reading it, and (b) pages were falling out of it. Some of us were starting to suspect that he wasn't a real pilot at all, but merely a man who had dressed up in a realistic pilot costume for Halloween. But we were desperate, so we followed him aboard yet another plane. As we taxied out to the runway, the pilot said—I swear—"Hopefully, this one will fly all the way."

6. So we took off from San Francisco, and for a while everything was fine except for the aroma coming from the seat behind us, which was occupied by a wretched woman who was attempting to get to Australia with two very small children, whom she evidently intended to enter in the World Pooping

MODERN AIRPORT DESIGN

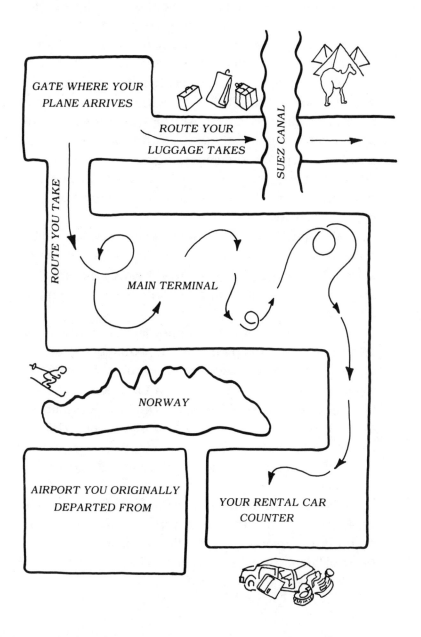

Championships. But this ceased to be our main concern when, after about an hour over the Pacific, which is famous for not having anyplace on it where you can land, the pilot announced that we had a "minor engine problem."

7. So we turned around and headed back toward, you guessed it, San Francisco, which we were beginning to think of as home. All the way back the pilot kept reassuring us about how *minor* this engine problem was, so you can imagine our excitement when we got to the airport and saw what appeared to be the entire San Francisco Fire Department lining the runway.

8. We landed safely and scuttled off the plane to be greeted, once again, by the devil, who was now being assisted by a witch. Of course by this point, Hell seemed like a major improvement over commercial air travel.

9. Several hours later our pilot led us onto yet *another* plane. By this point a lot of people had dropped out of the flight, but we were determined to see what would ultimately happen, with a lot of smart money betting that this would become the first commercial airliner ever to be sucked into a black hole. During the Preflight Safety Lecture—I swear this is true—the flight attendant said, "If you gotta go, go with a smile."

10. We took off from San Francisco again and flew back out over the Pacific, where, to judge from the amount of "turbulence," we flew smack into a whole *herd* of airborne water buffalo. The in-flight movie was *The Dead Poets Society*.

11. We landed in Honolulu, 21 hours after we left Miami. To apologize for our inconvenience, the flight attendants gave us coupons that were good for discounts on future flights, although they knew full well that we were all planning to return to the mainland via canoe.

I do not mean to suggest here that all flights take this long to reach their destinations. Some of them *never* reach their destinations. And I understand that there are even some, the ones that I personally am not on, that arrive right on schedule. You just never know, which is why air travel is the ongoing adventure that it is.

AIRPORT SECURITY

The important thing to remember about airport security procedures is that they have been created for *your protection*. Sure, it can be annoying to have to stop at the security checkpoint when you're on a tight schedule, but look at it this way: If the security personnel do their job properly, they just might cause you to *miss your plane*, thereby possibly saving your life.

The heart of the airport security system is the **metal detector**, a device that shoots invisible rays into your body. These rays are perfectly harmless, according to security personnel, although you notice that THEY never go through the metal detector. In fact, when nobody's around, they use it to cook their lunch. So most travel experts recommend that, to avoid turning your internal organs into baked lasagna, you go through the detector as fast as possible, maybe even back up fifty yards or so and get a running start.

The purpose of the metal detector is to make sure that you're not carrying a bomb or a deadly weapon or a set of car keys. If the detector detects one of these items, it will beep; security personnel will ask you to place the item on a plastic tray and go through the detector again. Your item will be returned to you on the other side ("Wait, sir! You forgot your bomb!").

How to Act While Going Through Security

Security personnel are on the lookout for people who fit the Profile of Suspected Terrorists, which is as follows:

PROFILE OF SUSPECTED TERRORISTS	
SEX	Male
AGE	15 through 74
LOOKS SUSPICIOUS?	Yes

As a smart traveler who wishes to avoid the inconvenience of being taken to a small airless interrogation room and having electrical wiring attached to your various genitals, you should make every effort to avoid fitting this profile. This means that if you are, for example, a male, you should try to deflect the security personnel's attention away from this fact via such techniques as:

- Wearing a dress.[2]
- Periodically remarking out loud to nobody in particular: "I certainly have a lot of body hair, for a woman!"

Baggage Searches

At the security checkpoint, your carry-on baggage must be placed on a conveyor belt and passed through an X-ray machine so the security personnel can see if you are carrying questionable items, because if you are, federal law requires them to open up your luggage and root around among your personal belongings like starving boars in a full Dumpster. If they find anything suspicious, For Your Own Protection they will ask you certain standard security questions, such as:

- "What's this stain in your underwear? Cheez Whiz?"
- "This is a *vibrator*? I never *seen* a vibrator this big! HEY, NORM! TAKE A LOOK AT THIS LADY'S VIBRATOR!"

---

[2]This is how Oliver North handles it

"For Kids Only": Fun with Airport Security Personnel

Airport security personnel are chosen for their sense of humor, and there is nothing they enjoy so much as a good joke. A fun game you kids can play with them is "Uncle Ted." What you do is, when you get near the security checkpoint, you walk up to a passenger selected at random and say in a loud voice, "Uncle Ted, can I see the bomb again?" Ha ha! Those wacky, fun-loving security personnel will sure come running! They might even take "Uncle Ted" for a ride in the electric cart! They might even take YOU for a ride in the electric cart if you mention the detonator in Mom's purse!

NOTE FROM THE PUBLISHER

—In this chapter Mr. Barry has been quite critical of commercial air travel, so we have decided, in the interest of fairness, to allow the airline industry an opportunity to respond. The following point-by-point rebuttal was written by Mr. M. Duane LeGrout, president of the American Association of Associated Airline Companies in Association with Each Other.

AN OPEN LETTER TO AIRLINE PASSENGERS
Dear Airline Passenger:

We will be starting this rebuttal in just a few moments.

Please remain in the area, as we are almost ready to start this point-by-point rebuttal. Thank you.

We apologize for the delay. We will begin rebutting very soon now, and we are grateful for your patience.

We have an announcement for those readers who are waiting for the point-by-point rebuttal. We are experiencing a minor equipment problem with our word processor at this time, but we do expect to have an announcement very soon and we do ask for your continued patience. In the meantime, we regret to announce that we have overbooked this rebuttal, and we are asking for readers who are willing to give up their space in exchange for an opportunity to read *two* future rebuttals on a topic of your choice. Thank you, and we expect to have another announcement shortly.

Okay, we do apologize for any inconvenience, but we have been informed that the word-processor problems have been corrected and we will begin rebutting any moment now. We ask that those of you with small shrieking children pLeAse asssidaisaas *(*^*&^^ hey can some-BoDy fiX thiS goddaM

REBUTTAL CANCELED SEE AGENT
Sincerely,

M. Duane LaGrout
President

Traveling as a Family

(OR: NO, WE ARE *NOT* THERE YET!)

*F*amily travel has been an American tradition ever since the days when hardy pioneer families crossed the Great Plains in oxen-drawn covered wagons, braving harsh weather, hostile Native Americans, unforgiving terrain, scarce food, and—worst of all— the constant whining coming from the backseat:

"Are we there yet?"

"Hey! THESE plains aren't so great!"

"Mom, Ezra is making hostile gestures at those Native Americans!"

"Are we almost there?"

"Mom! Rebecca dumped some unforgiving terrain into my scarce food!"

"PLEASE can we stop here and settle Kansas please please PLEASE??"

"Yuck! We're eating *bison* again?"

"When are we going to be there?"

"Mom! Little Ben put oxen poop in his hair!"

Yes, it was brutally hard, but those brave pioneers kept going, day after day, month after month, never stopping, and do you know why? Because *Dad was driving*, that's why. When Dad is driving, he never stops for *anything*. This is part of the Guy Code of Conduct. A lot of those early pioneer dads, when they got to California, drove their wagons directly into the Pacific Ocean and would probably have continued to Japan if it hadn't been for shark damage to the oxen.

Another part of the Guy Code of Conduct still in effect is that only Dad can drive. If necessary, Dad will permanently bond his hands to the steering wheel with Krazy Glue to prevent Mom from driving, because he knows that if she had the wheel, she might suffer a lapse of judgment and decide to actually *stop* for something, such as food or sleep or medical care for little Jennifer, whose appendix has apparently burst. No, Dad will not allow minor distractions such as these to interfere with his vacation schedule, which looks like this:

6:00–6:15 A.M.: **See Yellowstone National Park**
6:15–6:25 A.M.: **See Grand Canyon**
6:15–7:00 A.M.: **See Latin America**

What Dad means by "see," of course, is "drive past at 67 miles per hour." Dad feels it is a foolish waste of valuable vacation time to get out of the car and actually go *look* at an attraction such as the White House, Niagara Falls, the Louvre, etc.

I myself have been guilty of this behavior. Once we

were driving across the country and we got to South Dakota, a dirt-intensive state so sparsely populated that merely by entering it you automatically become a member of the legislature. A major tourist attraction in South Dakota is something called "Wall Drug," which is basically a group of stores advertised by a string of billboards that begins somewhere outside of the solar system. My wife, Beth, wanted to stop. Her reasoning was that we had driven hundreds of miles that day with absolutely no activity to relieve our boredom except eating Stuckey's miniature pecan pies at the rate of approximately three pies per person per hour. And so as we drew closer to Wall Drug, passing billboard after billboard—157 miles to go, 153 miles to go, 146 miles to go, etc.— her anticipation mounted, until finally we were there, and Beth's excitement reached a fever pitch because this was the only point of interest for hundreds, perhaps thousands, of miles, and of course I elected to *whiz right past it*, as though I had an important appointment elsewhere in South Dakota to pick up an urgent load of manure.

You know how certain incidents become permanent sore points in a marriage? Like for example a husband will never let his wife forget the time she left a $2,000 video camera where the baby could get hold of it and drop it into the toilet? That's the status that the Wall Drug Incident has achieved in our marriage. My wife feels that we're the only people in the history of interstate travel who failed to stop there, and, fifteen years later, she is still bitter. If she ever files for a divorce, this is the first incident she'll mention to the lawyer.

And that's the wonderful thing about family travel: it provides you with experiences that will remain locked forever in the scar tissue of your mind. Especially if you travel with children. We traveled extensively with our son Robert when he was very young, and I have many, many vivid memories of that period, all of which involve public rest rooms.

As you parents know, a small child can go for weeks without going to the bathroom at home, but once you hit the road, it becomes pretty much a full-time occupation. During my son Robert's early years, he and I visited just about every men's room on the East Coast. And if it was a really *disgusting* men's room, a men's room that contained the skeletons of Board of Health workers who died trying to inspect it, Robert would inevitably announce that he had to do Number Two.

So he'd go into a stall and close the door, and his little legs would disappear, and he'd remain there for as long as two days. God alone knows what he was doing in there. Meanwhile, of course, I'd stand guard outside the stall, because you can't leave a three-year-old alone. Inevitably strangers would come in, and there I'd be, apparently just hanging out alone in a men's room, and they'd look at me suspiciously. So in an effort to reassure these strangers that I was a Father on Duty, as opposed to some kind of lurking men's-room pervert, I'd try to strike up a conversation with Robert through the stall door:

ME: So, Robert, my three-year-old son who is inside this stall that I'm guarding as a responsible parent! How's it going in there?

STALL DOOR: (silence)
ME: Ha ha! Speak up, Robert!
STALL DOOR: (silence)

And the strangers would turn and stride quickly out the door, because nobody wants to be in a public rest room with a person who's talking to a toilet stall.

Of course, if there's anything more exciting than traveling with a child, it's traveling with *several* children. We ourselves have only one child, because after Beth experienced the Joy and Wonder of natural childbirth, she decided not to experience it again until modern science invents a method whereby the man has the contractions. But we have taken Robert's friends with us on numerous trips, and we have noted a phenomenon familiar to all parents, namely that you would have less conflict if you put the entire North and South Korean armed forces in your backseat than you get with just two children.

Children sitting in backseats are incapable of normal human conversation. Their conversational responses are all intended to raise the level of backseat hostility to the point where one party has no viable option but to spit Yoo-hoo into the other party's hair.

Examples

STATEMENT OF CHILD: Hey! I saw a horse!
RESPONSE OF NORMAL HUMAN: Where?
RESPONSE OF OTHER CHILD IN BACKSEAT: So what?
(Or: "You did not.")

STATEMENT OF CHILD: I like this song.
RESPONSE OF NORMAL HUMAN: That's nice.
RESPONSE OF OTHER CHILD IN BACKSEAT: So what?
(Or: "You do not.") (Or: "This song sucks.")

STATEMENT OF CHILD: In a right triangle, the square of the hypotenuse is equal to the sum of the squares of the other two sides.
RESPONSE OF NORMAL HUMAN: That is correct.
RESPONSE OF OTHER CHILD IN BACKSEAT: You suck.

One way to try to reduce the hostility level is to keep the children amused with Traditional Fun Car Games, such as watching for other cars' license plates and seeing who can find the one from the most distant state. This exciting activity is sure to captivate the children and provide hours of enjoyment ("I see one from Iowa!" "No you don't!" "So what?" "You suck!").

But for real family travel fun, there's no substitute for actually reaching some kind of destination. And the Number One family travel destination of all, as measured in total miles of people waiting in line, is of course:

THE WALT "YOU WILL HAVE FUN" DISNEY WORLD THEMED SHOPPING COMPLEX AND RESORT COMPOUND

I'm an expert on visiting Disney World, because we live only four hours away, and according to my records we spend about three-fifths of our after-tax income there. Not that I'm complaining. You can't have a bad time at Disney World. It's not *allowed*. They have hidden electronic surveillance cameras everywhere, and if they catch you failing to laugh with childlike wonder, they lock you inside a costume representing a beloved Disney character such as Goofy and make you walk around in the Florida heat getting grabbed and leaped on by violently excited children until you have learned your lesson. Yes, Disney World is a "dream vacation," and here are some tips to help make it "come true" for you!

When to Go: The best time to go, if you want to avoid huge crowds, is 1962.

How to Get There: It's possible to fly, but if you want the total Disney World experience, you should drive there with a minimum of four hostile children via the longest possible route. If you live in Georgia, for example, you should plan a route that includes Oklahoma.

Once you get to Florida, you can't miss Disney World, because the Disney corporation owns the entire center of the state (see map). Just get on any major highway, and eventually it will dead-end in a Disney parking area large enough to have its own climate, populated by large nomadic families who have been trying to find their cars since the Carter administration. Be sure to note carefully where you leave *your* car, because later on you may want to sell it so you can pay for your admission tickets.

But never mind the price; the point is that now you're finally *there*, in the ultimate vacation fantasy paradise, ready to have fun! Well, okay, you're not

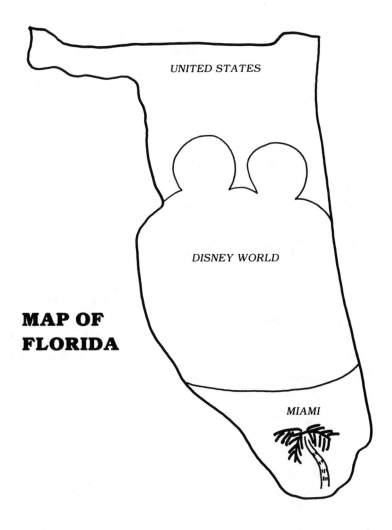

MAP OF FLORIDA

exactly there *yet*. First you have to wait for the parking-lot tram, driven by cheerful uniformed Disney employees, to come around and pick you up and give you a helpful lecture about basic tram-safety rules such as never fall out of the tram without coming to a full and complete stop.

But now the tram ride is over and it's time for fun! Right? Don't be an idiot. It's time to wait in line to buy admission tickets. Most experts recommend that you go with the 47-day pass, which will give you a chance, if you never eat or sleep, to visit *all* of the Disney themed attractions, including The City of the Future, The Land of Yesterday, The Dull Suburban Residential Community of Sometime Next Month, Wet Adventure, Farms on Mars, The World of Furniture, Sponge Encounter, the Nuclear Flute Orchestra, Appliance Island, and the Great Underwater Robot Hairdresser Adventure, to name just a few.

Okay, you've taken out a second mortgage and purchased your tickets! Now, finally, it's time to . . . wait in line again! This time, it's for the monorail, a modern, futuristic transportation system that whisks you to the Magic Kingdom at nearly half the speed of a lawn tractor. Along the way cheerful uniformed Disney World employees will offer you some helpful monorail-safety tips such as never set fire to the monorail without first removing your personal belongings.

And now, at last, you're at the entrance to the Magic Kingdom itself! No more waiting in line for transportation! It's time to *wait in line to get in.* Wow! Look at all the *other* people waiting to get in! There are tour groups here with names like "Entire Population of Indiana." There sure must be some great attractions inside these gates!

And now you've inched your way to the front of the line, and the cheerful uniformed Disney employee is stamping your hand with a special invisible chemical that penetrates your nervous system and causes you to temporarily acquire the personality of a cow. "Moo!" you shout as you surge forward with the rest of the herd.

And now, unbelievably, you're actually inside the Magic Kingdom! At last! Mecca! You crane your head to see over the crowd around you, and with innocent childlike wonder you behold: *a much larger crowd.* Ha ha! You are having some kind of fun now!

And now you are pushing your way forward, thrusting other vacationers aside, knocking over their strollers if necessary, because little Jason wants to ride on Space Mountain. Little Jason has been talking about Space Mountain ever since Oklahoma, and by God you're going to take him on it, no matter how long the . . . My God! Can *this* be the line for Space Mountain? This line is so long that there are Cro-Magnon families at the front! Perhaps if you explain to little Jason that he could be a deceased old man by the time he gets on the actual ride, he'll agree to skip it and . . . NO! Don't scream, little Jason! We'll just purchase some official Mickey Mouse sleeping bags, and we'll stay in line as long as it takes! The hell with third grade! We'll just stand here and chew our cuds! Mooooo!

Speaking of education, you should be sure to visit Epcot Center, which features exhibits sponsored by large corporations showing you how various challenges facing the human race are being met and overcome thanks to the selfless efforts of large corporations. Epcot Center also features pavilions built by various foreign nations, where you can experience an extremely realistic simulation of what life in these nations would be like if they consisted almost entirely of restaurants and souvenir stores.

One memorable Epcot night my family and I ate at the German restaurant, where I had several large beers and a traditional German delicacy called "Bloatwurst," which is a sausage that can either be eaten or used as a tackling dummy. When we got out I felt like one of those snakes that eat a cow whole and then just lie around and digest it for a couple of months. But my son was determined to go on a new educational Epcot ride called "The Body," wherein you sit in a compartment that simulates what it would be like if you got inside a spaceship-like vehicle and got shrunk down to the size of a gnat and got injected inside a person's body.

I'll tell you what it's like: awful. You're looking at a screen showing an extremely vivid animated simulation of the human interior, which is not the most appealing way to look at a human unless you're attracted to white blood cells the size of motor homes. Meanwhile the entire compartment is bouncing you around violently, especially when you go through the aorta. "Never go through the aorta after eating German food," that is my new travel motto.

What gets me is, I waited in line for an *hour* to do this. I could have experienced essentially the same level of enjoyment merely by sticking my finger down my throat.

Which brings me to my idea for getting rich. No doubt you have noted that, in most amusement parks, the popularity of a ride is directly proportional to how horrible it is. There's hardly ever a line for nice, relaxing rides like the merry-go-round. But there will always be a huge crowd, mainly consisting of teenagers, waiting to go on a ride with a name like "The Dicer," where they strap people into what is essentially a giant food processor and turn it on and then phone the paramedics.

So my idea is to open up a theme park called "Dave World," which will have a ride called "The Fall of Death." This will basically be a 250-foot tower. The way it will work is, you climb to the top, a trapdoor opens up, and you splat onto the asphalt below like a bushel of late-summer tomatoes.

Obviously, for legal reasons, I couldn't let anybody actually *go* on this ride. There would be a big sign that said:

WARNING!
NOBODY CAN GO ON THIS RIDE.
THIS RIDE IS INVARIABLY FATAL,
THANK YOU.

But this would only make The Fall of Death more popular. Every teenager in the immediate state would come to Dave World just to stand in line for it.

Dave World would also have an attraction called "ParentLand," which would have a sign outside that said: "Sorry, Kids! This Attraction Is for Mom 'n' Dad Only!" Inside would be a bar. For younger children, there would be "Soil Fantasy," a themed play area consisting of dirt or, as a special "rainy-day" bonus, mud.

I frankly can't see how Dave World could fail to become a huge financial success that would make me rich and enable me to spend the rest of my days traveling the world with my family. So the hell with it.

Seeing Other Attractions in the Disney World Area

You must be very careful here. You must sneak out of Disney World in the dead of night, because the Disney people do *not* want you leaving the compound and spending money elsewhere. If they discover that you're gone, cheerful uniformed employees led by Mickey Mouse's lovable dog Pluto, who will sniff the ground in a comical manner, will track you down. And when they catch you, it's *into the Goofy suit.*

So we're talking about a major risk, but it's worth it for some of the attractions around Disney World. The two best ones, as it happens, are right next to each other near a town called Kissimmee. One of them is the world headquarters of the Tupperware company, where you can take a guided tour that includes a Historic Food Containers Museum. I am not making this up.

I am also not making up Gatorland, which is next door. After entering Gatorland through a giant pair of pretend alligator jaws, you find yourself on walkways over a series of murky pools in which are floating a large number of alligators that appear to be recovering from severe hangovers, in the sense that they hardly ever move. You can purchase fish to feed them, but the typical Gatorland alligator will ignore a fish even if it lands directly on its head. Sometimes you'll see an alligator, looking bored, wearing three or four rotting, fly-encrusted fish, like some kind of High Swamp Fashion headgear.

This is very entertaining, of course, but the *real* action at Gatorland, the event that brings even the alligators to life, is the Assault on the Dead Chickens, which is technically known as the Gator Jumparoo. I am also not making this up. The way it works is, a large crowd of tourists gathers around a central pool, over which, suspended from wires, are a number of plucked headless chicken carcasses. As the crowd, encouraged by the Gatorland announcer, cheers wildly, the alligators lunge out of the water and rip the chicken carcasses down with their jaws. Once you've witnessed this impressive event, you will never again wonder how America got to be the country that it is today.

And speaking of America, let's talk about taking the children to one of this nation's many fine:

EDUCATIONAL HISTORIC SITES

Forget it. Your modern child is not interested in educational historic sites. Your modern child has grown up with MTV and Nintendo; he or she is not going to be enthralled by watching people in authentic uncomfortable colonial outfits demonstrate how families in 1750 used to make candles by spinning flax with a churn, or whatever the hell they did. So you should avoid this kind of activity. Also you should avoid stopping at those Historical Markers on the side of the highway that you can never read when you're driving past because the letters are too small. Here's what they say:

HISTORIC MARKER

This Historic Marker was erected on this site in the Year of Our Lord 1923 during the administration of Governor Rayford R. "Scooter" Grommet, Jr., to commemorate with great sadness the numerous innocent civilians who are almost definitely going to get hit by traffic when they stop their cars and get out and try to read these really tiny letters.

TRAVELING WITH TEENAGERS

Traveling with teenagers is somewhat more difficult than traveling with members of the actual human race. It's very important for you to be sensitive to the fact that, during this difficult transition from child to adult, your teenagers are undergoing intense emotional stresses that cause them, for solid psychological reasons, to regard you as the biggest geek ever to roam the planet. This is because a teenager's life is an extremely intense, impossibly complex drama, and you cannot possibly understand the plot. All you can do is blunder around like some kind of nearsighted elephant, making a mess of *everything*, including the seemingly simple act of asking a passing waitress for ketchup.

YOU: Waitress, could we please have some ketchup?

YOUR TEENAGED DAUGHTER: Oh FATHER! How COULD you?? *(Crying, she rushes from the restaurant.)*

YOU: What did I do? What did I do?

YOUR OTHER DAUGHTER *(in the tone of voice you might use to address an ax murderer)*: What did you DO? Do you realize who you just asked for ketchup?

YOU: A waitress?

YOUR OTHER DAUGHTER: That was *Jennifer Wienerbunker*! The captain of the cheerleading squad! You asked her for *ketchup*.

YOU *(raising your voice slightly)*: But she's a *waitress*.

YOUR OTHER DAUGHTER: Oh FATHER! *(Crying, she rushes from the restaurant.)*

Also, teenagers are bored. By everything. Show a teenager an actual volcanic eruption, in progress, featuring giant billowing clouds of smoke, hot rocks raining from the sky, lava flows destroying entire villages, etc., and the teenager, eyebrows arched with sarcasm, will look at you and say, "Gee, this is *swell*," then return to the rental car, turn on his portable CD player, and listen to a band called Stomach Contents.

So as a parent, you may feel that your wisest course is to postpone your family traveling until your teenage child has reached a more reasonable age, such as forty-eight. If this is not possible, you'll want to follow the:

Two Major Rules for Traveling with Teenagers

1. **Always Remain Outside of the Embarrassment Zone.** If you get too close to your teenager in public, your teenager will become concerned that *other* teenagers might think that your teenager was somehow *connected* with you, which of course would be hideously embarrassing. So while traveling you must always maintain the Minimum Acceptable Public Distance, as shown in this figure:

COLORADO	KANSAS
Denver	Wichita
o==================o	

Minimum Acceptable Distance Between Parent and Teenaged Child in Public

2. **Find Activities That Are Interesting to Teenagers.** If the teenager is bored with an activity that you have planned, simply select an activity that he or she might find more interesting. Here is a handy chart to help you do this:

ACTIVITY THAT WOULD BE BORING FOR TEENAGER	ALTERNATIVE ACTIVITY THAT MIGHT BE MORE IN-TERESTING FOR TEENAGER
Visiting the Louvre Museum	Leaving the Louvre Museum
Seeing the Crown Jewels	Not Seeing the Crown Jewels
Touring India by Elephant	Anyplace but India. *Definitely* Not on an Elephant.

See the USA First!

(WHILE WE STILL OWN PART OF IT)

As Americans, we are fortunate to live in a large nation[1] of incredible variety, as is so eloquently described in the moving opening lines of "America the Beautiful":

> **Well East Coast girls are hip,**
> **I really dig those styles they wear.**

Yes, this is a land of rich diversity, from the towering skyscrapers of Manhattan all the way to the towering mounds of garbage piled up *next* to the towering skyscrapers of Manhattan, and you owe it to yourself, as an American, to see it all. Why go to

[1] America

Europe, with its high prices and strange food and incomprehensible lingos, when, with just a little effort, you can find those things right here?

To help you get the most out of your "American Adventure," we've prepared the following state-by-state breakdown of Useful Facts and Tips. The information for this section was obtained via an exhaustive process of typing the name of a state and then trying to remember if we or anybody we knew had ever been there. Also, we got a lot of useful information from our son's encyclopedia, a handy reference work that we always carry along when we travel, which is why we need a back operation.

THE FIFTY STATES
Alabama

Often called "The Pancreas of Dixie," Alabama offers a tremendous amount of culture as well as turnips. The State Flower is the camelia; the State Dog is named "Booger" and you should not wake him up. Montgomery, Alabama, was the first capital of the Confederacy and in 1861 was the site of the inauguration of legendary Civil War coach Paul "Bear" Bryant. Many other fascinating historic and cultural events have also occurred in this dynamic state. Ask around.

Alaska

Despite being close to Alabama in the encyclopedia, Alaska is actually located in Canada. This is only one of the astounding facts about this dynamic state, which is so big that if you were to walk across it at the rate of 25 miles per day, you would get moose poop all over your shoes. You find moose poop *everywhere* in Alaska. You can buy souvenirs made from it. We once bought (this is true) some moose-poop swizzle sticks in Alaska's largest city, Anchorage, where our hotel had a huge stuffed bear in the lobby striking a pose that said: "Welcome to Alaska! I am going to rip your face off!" Alaska also contains large quantities of nature in the form of tundra ("tundra" is the Eskimo word for "nothing") and glaciers, which are enormous pieces of ice that have somehow developed the ability to creep around, which is a pretty scary concept and we just hope that they don't learn to walk erect. The Official State Motto of Alaska is: "Brrrrrrr!" The Official State Bird is covered with oil.

Arizona

When you think of Arizona, you naturally think of one of the great wonders of the world, a spectacular natural formation carved out of the rock over millions of years by the Colorado River, namely: Niagara Falls. But this dynamic state also features the subtler beauty of the desert ("desert" is a Spanish word meaning "tundra"), home of the scorpion, which is the Official State Creature That Crawls into Your Shoe and Can Cause Paralysis. Another popular attraction is London Bridge, which was transported stone by stone from England hidden in the luggage of a group of very aggressive souvenir-seeking Arizonans on a European tour. They would have got more, but a suspicious British airport security employee opened one of their carry-on bags and discovered a large segment of Stonehenge.

Arkansas

With its ideal location somewhere in the United States that we can never quite picture in our mind, Arkansas offers convenient access to adjoining regions, plus a football team whose fans wear masks with giant hog snouts (at least we *assume* those are masks). It is little wonder that millions of visitors flock to this dynamic state each year, purchase gasoline, and continue flocking on through. Among the many fascinating historic events that have occurred in Arkansas are the Louisiana Purchase, bauxite, and Hernando de Soto. Also Arkansas once elected a governor named "Orval E. Faubus." The Official State Egg Order is "over medium."

California

The nation's most populous state, California truly lives up to its dynamic nickname, "The Nation's Most Populous State," with enough uniformed parking valets in Los Angeles alone to conquer Eastern Europe. Southern California also boasts more than 57 billion convenient miles of freeway and many fascinating places to visit, although we frankly have no idea which exit you take to get to them. But you should definitely try to find Universal Studios, where you can get a "behind-the-scenes" look at an actual working amusement park, including a terrifying ride where, in the climactic finale, you are attacked by a realistic fourteen-ton animated replica of Zsa Zsa Gabor.

Visitors to Northern California will definitely want to visit Wine Country, where they can snork down a couple dozen free samples and then go experience the dry heaves amidst the awesome towering grandeur of the giant redwoods, which are the oldest living things on Earth that are not members of the Grateful Dead. And of course no trip to Northern California would be complete without a visit to San Francisco, whose romantic charm inspired the immortal Tony Bennett song, "Don't Mess with My Toot Toot." Be sure to join several tons of carbohydrate-bloated tourists for a ride on a quaint cable car, lurching up quaint "hills" that are actually 800-foot vertical drops as the cable-car driver dings the quaint little bell, sending out the cheerful message "ding-a-ding-ding," which is code for: "Look out, my cable is badly frayed."

California's State Blender Setting is puree.

Colorado

Besides being dynamic, Colorado is best known for the breathtaking beauty of the Rocky Mountains, which are still visible in some areas peeking out from under a dense protective layer of condominium units.

It's no wonder that each year millions of skiers come to experience the state's superb emergency medical facilities! Colorado is also rich in minerals, but so what? is our feeling. The capital and largest city is Denver, which needless to say boasts museums, symphonies, etc. You have probably noticed that virtually *all* cities, including some real armpits, like to boast that they have museums and symphonies, which are of course the *last* things that you, the typical visitor, really want at the end of a hard day of traveling. What you want is a motel room that doesn't have hairs on the sheets. The Colorado State Garnish is parsley.

Connecticut

Connecticut, often referred to as "The Nutmeg State" by people who have confused it with Vermont, is famous for being dynamic and containing Yale University, where in 1889 (we are not making this up) the tackling dummy[2] was invented. The state capital, Hartford, is the headquarters of many large insurance companies, so keep your car doors locked. Also be sure to visit Mystic Seaport, where you can see an actual whaling ship in which courageous nineteenth-century mariners went to sea to do battle with monstrous fourteen-ton animated replicas of Zsa Zsa Gabor. Connecticut's Official State Prank is the whoopee cushion.

[2] Or "bloatwurst" (see Chapter Four)

Delaware

Delaware was the first state to ratify the U.S. Constitution, thereby earning it the proud nickname, "The Nutmeg State." Although small in size, Delaware has had a major impact on the nation's destiny: Thomas Jefferson, Abraham Lincoln, Franklin Roosevelt, and John F. Kennedy all traveled through or flew over Delaware at some time or another, as far as we know. Delaware also boasts dynamism and several million chickens. Reservations are recommended.

Florida

This happens to be our place of residence, and we are not just "tooting our own horn" when we say that no other state offers as many dynamic opportunities to encounter gigantic insects. We have cockroaches here that, instead of scuttling under a counter when you flick on the kitchen light, will pick up your entire refrigerator and lumber from the room. Also in the nature department we have the Everglades, an extremely fascinating natural swamp that inevitably causes the first-time visitor to exclaim: "Huh." The major state industries are tourism, Bingo, obtaining senior-citizen discounts, and not having automobile insurance. The state capital is Epcot Center. The largest city is Miami (official tourism slogan: "Maybe You Won't Get Shot"), a richly diverse cosmopolitan metropolis where people from many different cultures live and work together while continuing to observe the traffic laws of their individual countries of origin. The Florida State Seal depicts a mosquito carrying a machine gun.

Georgia

Although much of Georgia was burned down during the filming of *Gone With the Wind*, this dynamic state has rebuilt itself and is now an important part of the "New South" (which is similar to the Old South, except most of the pickup trucks are Japanese). Georgia's biggest city, Atlanta, proudly boasts that it has "the nation's busiest airport," although frankly this strikes us as an odd thing to boast about, comparable to announcing that you have the nation's largest epidemic of crotch lice. Other major tourist attractions include some big rocks and a great many pine trees that can be seen engaging in photosynthesis, the Official State Chemical Reaction. Georgia is also the proud host of the world-famous Masters Golf Tournament of Champions Wearing Ugly Pants, although of course you personally are not invited.

Hawaii

Visitors to this dynamic island paradise are sure to be greeted by a friendly "Aloha," the all-purpose Hawaiian word that means "Hello," "Good-bye," "I love you," "I hate you," and "Give me the fish of your brother Raoul." Geologically, the Hawaiian island chain was formed when volcanoes on the floor of the Pacific Ocean spewed out molten lava, which eventually cooled off and formed large resort hotel complexes. These in turn attracted hardy Polynesian mariners, who traveled thousands of miles in open canoes, braving fierce storms that washed all of their consonants overboard, so they arrived in the Hawaiian Islands with a language consisting almost entirely of vowels, the result being that all the traffic signs say things like KA'IIU'UAEIA'AA STREET. The modern Hawaiian economy consists of pineapples and pineapple-shaped tourists wearing comical shirts and watching authentic performances of the hula, in which dancers use traditional arm gestures to tell the story of how their ancestors, thousands of years ago, used to make various gestures with their arms. The Official State Motto is "Wai'iu'a'iou'lih'aaaine," but nobody has any idea what it means.

Idaho

Idaho is probably best known for being the state where my wife, Beth, ate an entire strawberry pie in a diner parking lot. This occurred in 1974 when we were driving across the country and found ourselves in a city called "Pocatello," which had a sign that made the proud boast:

POCATELLO
"Crossroads of the Interstates"

So we stopped at a diner there and ate a huge breakfast. We eat a lot on long trips because we feel our bodies are less likely to become bored if they can pass the time converting food into fat. We plan our itinerary around meals ("Do you want to see the Grand Canyon?" "Does it have a snack bar?"), and our travel memories tend to focus on food to the exclusion of all other factors ("Remember Asia?" "Yes! Those little fish rolls!").

So we ate a vast breakfast at this diner, and on our way out Beth noticed that they had fresh-baked strawberry pies for sale, and so naturally she bought one, her reasoning being that Idaho was basically still a wilderness area and there might not be any other food in it. Her plan was to save the pie until we really desperately needed it, say in fifteen miles or so, but when we got into our car, she decided she'd better sample it, in case it was defective. I was maneuvering the car out of the parking space, and I heard this unusual noise—a combination of ecstatically passionate moan and industrial vacuum cleaner—and when I looked over, the entire pie was *gone*. Vanished, before we even got to the street. Seventeen years later, the memory of that pie still brings a dynamic sparkle to Beth's eye that is rarely there when she looks at me, or even Kevin Costner. Idaho's Official State Chemical Element is helium.

Illinois

Illinois is "The Land of Lincoln," and the memory of "Honest Abe" is so deeply revered there that as recently as 1983 he was elected lieutenant governor. Illinois is also the nation's largest soybean-producing state, although nobody knows what happens to the soybeans after they're grown. You never see them for sale. We think the farmers just harvest them and throw them away.

The largest city in Illinois is, of course, Chicago, which proudly refers to itself as "The City with a Great Big Butt." This dynamic metropolis began as a tiny trading post in the 1600s, when trappers would paddle canoes filled with animal pelts down the Chicago River, then throw them into Lake Michigan, because by then they smelled awful. During World War II scientists started the first controlled nuclear reaction at the University of Chicago. At least it has been under control *so far*. Some days it gets a little frisky, which is why a lot of smart Illinois residents also maintain residences in Guam. Today Chicago boasts the Sears Tower, which is so tall that occupants on the top floor sometimes have to phone the street level to find out what the weather's like "down there"! These occupants have had a *lot* to drink.

Indiana

Indiana is a country in Southeast Asia consisting of more than 13,600 islands. No! Wait! We're looking at the encyclopedia article for Ind*onesia*. Ind*iana* is located in the Midwest and consists of *less* than 13,600 islands. It is called "The Hoosier State," after the sound that pigs make when they sneeze. Another dynamic activity that occurs there is the exciting Indianapolis 500, where each year the world's top racing-car drivers roar around the legendary Indianapolis Speedway, again and again until the excitement and tension become so great that you have to change the channel and watch *Celebrity Turkey Basting*.[3] Indiana also boasts higher education and Historic Fort Wayne, where men dressed in authentic old soldier costumes engage in authentic soldier activities and, if they are not careful, contract various authentic diseases. Abraham Lincoln also lived in Indiana for a while, but he moved. The Official State Semi-Obscure Adjective is "febrile."

Iowa

Iowa's Official State Motto is "You Bet," which is what everybody there automatically says in response to any question:

PREACHER: Do you take this man to be your lawful wedded husband, even if he gets sick, or becomes poor, or brings home a dog that throws up a semi-digested mole head in your lingerie drawer?

IOWA BRIDE: You bet.

Iowa produces dynamic quantities of pork. The other major industry is making fun of people from Minnesota, who have a big rivalry with the Iowans, although even scientists using sophisticated instruments cannot tell the two groups apart. Iowa also offers plenty of culture: In fact, the very name of the

[3] Host: Wink Martindale

state capital, Des Moines, is French. It means "some of these Moines." Iowa's Official State Local Boy Who Went on to Become a Famous Dead Movie Star is John Wayne, whose birthplace is open to the public. We strongly recommend that you stop for a visit, although we personally shot past it at nearly 80 miles per hour.

Kansas

Although it is now covered with agriculture, Kansas was at one time very historic. It was the on-scene location of the "Wild West," where "longhorns" riding "six-shooters" used to "rustle up" some "varmints." This era eventually ended due to a shortage of quotation marks, but Kansans are still proud of their state's rough-and-tumble tradition, and will often greet a stranger by warmly breaking a chair over his head. Kansas also contains manufacturing and tumbleweeds, which are plants that form themselves into giant balls that roll across the prairie and burst into your motel room at night, which is why the American Automobile Association recommends that you always sleep with a weed whacker.

Kentucky

Kentucky is best known as the state where sleek racehorses drink bourbon whiskey and smoke the legendary "bluegrass" tobacco, then compete for the honor of wearing the famous "Kentucky Derby."

Kentucky also leads the nation in the production of bituminous coal, which is especially valuable because it has two tuminouses. The coal industry is very tourist-oriented, and members of the public are welcome to strip vast quantities of irreplaceable topsoil and take it home with them. Another "must-see" in Kentucky is Fort Knox, which offers guided tours daily from nine A.M. until five P.M. to all visitors who make it across the mine field. You may also want to visit Mammoth Cave, which is an incredibly beautiful and dynamic natural formation, although unfortunately you can't actually *see* anything because it's located underground. The Kentucky State Pruning Implement is shears.

Louisiana

Louisiana was discovered by the Cajuns, a dynamic group of people who came down from Canada and decided to stay after they forgot where they had parked. This kind of thing happens a lot in Louisiana, especially in the state capital, New Orleans, where the Official Motto is: "Laissez les bons temps rouler." ("Look out, I'm about to throw up.") New Orleans is a wide-open town, a town where there is gambling and cursing and heavy drinking and naked dancing and wild orgiastic sex. And that's just in the *police station.* The rest of the city is even looser, especially the French Quarter, which is so decadent that if the Reverend Jerry Falwell were to merely walk down the length of Bourbon Street, he would emerge at the other end with an overpowering desire to purchase leather underwear.[4] New Orleans also boasts a number of historic sites, the major one being Nick G. Castrogiovanni's Original Big Train Bar, which is where, during the 1988 Republican convention, this author, for sound journalism reasons, drank a drink called "A Wild Night at the Capri Motel" out of a large styrofoam container shaped like a toilet.

CORRECTION:

We have been informed that New Orleans is not the state capital of Louisiana. New Orleans is the state capital of Utah. We regret the error.

Maine

During the warm season (August 8 and 9), Maine is a true "vacation paradise," offering visitors a chance to jump into crystal-clear mountain lakes and see if they can get back out again before their bodily tissue is frozen as solid as a supermarket turkey. This dynamic climate has produced a hardy stock of local residents who at first seem a bit "standoffish," although when you take the time to get to know them, you will discover that many of them are actually dead. A major tourist attraction in Maine is Kenneth

---

[4] Assuming he doesn't have some already

E. Bunkport IV, the quaint seaside town where George Bush, who is a fiend for recreation, often goes to throw horseshoes at fish from his golf cart. Maine also features numerous fascinating pine trees as well as an average annual precipitation. The Official State Boxed Movie Refreshment is Milk Duds.

Maryland

Maryland is a fast-growing state boasting a dynamic economy based on giving speeding tickets to people attempting to drive through. One of Maryland's major attractions is the Chesapeake Bay, a crab-intensive body of water that gets its name from the Indian word "Cesapiq," which means "Chesapeake." Maryland also contains Baltimore, site of the historic Fort McHenry, where in 1812 Francis Scott Key wrote "The Star-Spangled Banner" to express the joy he felt after watching the Orioles defeat the Yankees in a critical American League East game. Maryland also boasts the nation's first umbrella factory. Sometimes Maryland gets positively *obnoxious*, boasting about this. You'll go to a bar where states hang out, and there will be Maryland, after about six shots of Wild Turkey, shouting, "Oh YEAH? Well you, wanna know who had the FIRST UMBRELLA FACTORY? Huh? LISTEN TO ME WHEN I'M TALKING TO YOU!" The Official State Sport of Maryland—we swear we are not making this one up, and we urge you to look it up if you don't believe us—is jousting.

Massachusetts

Massachusetts (also an Indian word, meaning "place that is hard to spell") is one of the most historic states in the union, which is why each year tens of thousands of visitors flock here, only to be killed in traffic. In Boston, the drivers refuse to obey even the laws of *physics*. This is the only place in the United States where the Driver's Manual actually *shows you how to give people the finger.*[5]

But potential death is a small price to pay for the opportunity to visit the many Massachusetts historic sites that played such a vital role in the formation of our nation—sites such as Plymouth Rock, where the Pilgrims, grateful to have survived a difficult three-month sea crossing, knelt to throw up; and the steeple of the Old North Church, from which silversmith Paul Revere flashed the message that started the Revolutionary War ("Your silverware order is not ready yet"). Massachusetts is also the site of the nation's first college, Harvard, which for more than three centuries has produced graduates who, no matter what their philosophical differences, are all dedicated to the lofty goal of subtly letting you know that they went to Harvard. They never mention it directly. What they do is constantly work the name "Cambridge" into the conversation. You'll say "Nice day," and they'll say "Yes! We had days like this in Cambridge!" Or you'll say "Pass the salt," and they'll say "Certainly! I used to pass the salt in Cam-

[5] Rim shot

bridge!'' The major industries of Massachusetts are having comical accents and expecting the Red Sox to screw up.

Michigan

Michigan is best known for being the place where, in 1896, Henry Ford built the first commercially successful automobile, using parts manufactured by the Toyota Corporation. This resulted in Detroit, a modern dynamic city that is well worth flying over at a minimum altitude of seven miles. Michigan also contains the Great Lakes, five mighty bodies of water— Lake Michigan, Lake Superior, Lake Toledo, Lake Inferior, and the Mayor Earl T. Wonkerman Memorial Lake—which inspired the great eighteenth-century poet Henry Wadsworth Allan Poe to write the immortal "Song of Hiawatha":

By the shores of Gitche Gumee;
By the shining Big-Sea water;
Strode the mighty Hiawatha;
In a frock he made from otter.
(Chorus)

Speaking of culture, the *World Book Encyclopedia* states that every year Michigan has a "Magic Get-Together" in a city named "Colon." We definitely think you should check this out.

Minnesota

Minnesota has more than 10,000 lakes, which has earned it the proud nickname: "The Gopher State." The major industries are (1) cows and (2) trying to get cars started, which is very difficult because the entire state is located inside the Arctic Circle. The largest and most dynamic city is Minneapolis (nickname: "St. Paul"), which boasts culture and some nice malls. Also there is a state fair where people make realistic sculptures entirely out of butter. And while you're in Minnesota, be sure to take the whole family on the tour of the world-famous Mayo Clinic, where every visitor receives a free "take-home" souvenir spleen transplant. Minnesota's Official State Office Supply is staples.

Mississippi

Mississippi has been unfairly portrayed in movies and TV shows as a backward, poorly educated state where the average resident has seventeen teeth and rides around in a pickup truck with a shotgun and a mongrel dog that scores higher on the SAT tests than the average resident. This is a terribly unfair stereotype. The actual truth is closer to nineteen teeth. No! Ha ha! We're just kidding, Mississippi residents! Seriously, Mississippi is a dynamic and growing state, and many modern technological corporations are relocating there to take advantage of the ready availability of okra. Also Elvis was born in Tupelo, where you can visit his birthplace and possibly meet him in person. You'll also want to visit one of the old planta-

provided by a man named Darrel Rafferty, owner of Raffety's Fishbait Company, which sells tubes filled with maggots for bait. So one day a customer was in the Town Club Bar, complaining to Raffety that he didn't get enough maggots in his tube, so Raffety said, okay, show me—even though this was not his Official State Motto—and so the customer poured his maggots out on the bar, and some of the more dynamic ones started crawling away, and eureka,[6] the idea of racing maggots to raise money for charity was born. They built a maggot racecourse and took bets and everything. We spoke to the Town Club owner, Phil Schneider, and he said they'd hold more races if tourists came around and created a popular demand. So we definitely recommend that you make this your first Montana stop. Don't set your food down on the bar.

Other Montana attractions include nature and the headquarters of the world's largest intercontinental ballistic missile complex, where tourists are welcome to come in and spin the big "Select-a-Target" wheel.

Nebraska

Although it is usually thought of as a farm state, Nebraska boasts two area codes, 402 and 308, as well as the National Museum of Roller Skating, which is in Lincoln and is, shockingly, the *only museum in the world dedicated solely to roller skating*. Ne-

---

[6] Greek, meaning "They probably had a few beers in them"

tions, where attractive hostesses dressed in authentic costumes explain the old traditional lifestyle and flog an authentic motorized replica of a slave. Mississippi's Official State Motto is ''Whoooo-EEEEE!''

Missouri

Missouri is called ''The Show-Me State,'' because that was the winner of the Dumbest State Nickname Contest, narrowly edging out ''The Nanny Nanny Boo-Boo State.'' The largest city is St. Louis, which features a 630-foot-tall stainless-steel arch, a monument to the early pioneers who came west with nothing but their wagons, their guns, their dreams, and their 630-foot-tall stainless-steel arches. Visitors may ride to the top of the arch, where, high above the Mississippi River, they will experience the thrill of wanting really badly to get the hell back down on the ground. At least that was how we felt. You'll also want to go to visit Hannibal, the boyhood home of Samuel Clemens, who grew up, adopted a pen name, and became one of Missouri's, and America's, most beloved characters: Harry Truman. Missouri is also dynamic.

Montana

When we think of Montana, the tourist attraction that of course immediately leaps into our minds is the maggot races at the Town Club Bar in Three Forks. We are not making these races up. The maggots are

braska is also the only state in the union with a "uni-cameral" legislature, defined as "a legislature that bears its young underwater." But Nebraska was not always a bed of roses. When the first settlers arrived, they found a harsh, unforgiving place, a vast, tree-less expanse of barren, drought-parched soil. And so, summoning up the dynamic pioneer spirit of hope and steely determination, they left. But a few of them remained and built sod houses, which are actually made from dirt. Think about that. You can't *clean* a sod house, because it would be *gone*. The early set-tler parents had a hell of a time getting this through to their children. "You kids stop tracking dirt out of the house!" they'd yell. Nebraska's Official State Weakness is fudge.

Nevada

Let's get one thing straight: There is more to Nevada than just Las Vegas. There is also the part that you have to drive through to *get* to Las Vegas. Fortu-nately you can do this at upward of 130 miles per hour, because there is no speed limit in Nevada. In fact there are no laws at all in Nevada. Even murder is legal, but it rarely happens, because people get dis-tracted. A guy will be on his way to kill somebody, and he'll pass a slot machine, and he'll figure, what the heck, so he'll put in a quarter, and pretty soon he's broke and has to pawn his gun to get more quar-ters. The result is that Nevada has a very dynamic economy, with gambling being the number-one in-dustry, followed closely by blood donorship. Las Vegas is also a cultural center, featuring extravagant theatrical productions in which world-class performers express the artistic concept: "Get a load of these hooters." And *definitely* do not miss the Liberace Museum, which presents a fascinating piano-oriented view of history. One plaque reads: "With Abraham Lincoln as president, the Civil War was raging when the Steinway Company of New York created this fine piano made of solid rosewood." We can just imagine the scene at the Steinway Company that fateful day: The board of directors is seated around the conference table, grim-faced, and the chairman says, "Gentlemen, Abraham Lincoln is president, and the Civil War is raging! We must make a fine piano of solid rosewood!"

Nevada is also a Mecca for lovers of fine concrete, who will want to visit the Hoover Dam, which was completed in 1936 and resulted in the formation of the Grand Canyon. There is a guided tour of the dam, which your children will surely want to take seventeen or eighteen consecutive times while you go back to Vegas and shoot some craps.

New Hampshire

New Hampshire (formerly Vermont) contains many rustic little villages with names like "East Thwackmore" featuring quaint little inns where the harried visitor can escape from the high-pressure modern world, with its pesky flush toilets and central heating. New Hampshire is also the home of the famous New England town meeting, a dynamic example of "democracy in action" wherein once a year all the residents of each town gather to lick syrup off each other's thighs. One of New Hampshire's most popular attractions is the famous "Old Man of the Mountains," a natural granite formation that, when viewed from a certain angle, looks like rocks. New Hampshire's Official State Onion Dip Enhancer is chives.

New Jersey

New Jersey—nicknamed "The New Jersey Turnpike State"—boasts the nation's densest population and convenient access to a number of important bridges and tunnels. It's also a dynamic summer playground, drawing millions of visitors each year to attractions such as Atlantic City, one of the few seaside resorts that would actually be improved by the arrival of an oil slick. Among New Jersey's many historic sites is Giants Memorial Stadium, erected to mark the burial location of Jimmy Hoffa; visitors are welcome to come place a wreath on his memorial goalposts. The Revolutionary War also occurred in New Jersey, where on Christmas night, 1776, George Washington crossed the Delaware River near Trenton and, in one of the great surprise maneuvers in the history of warfare, found a decent restaurant. New Jersey's Official State Disease is gout.

New Mexico

New Mexico offers many fascinating and dynamic attractions that you will want to see before you run out of water and die. For example, you should definitely check out the Native American heritage. If you see some Native Americans, you just say, "Hey! Would you Native Americans mind posing for some pictures here? I got it! How about if you pretend that you're trying to scalp Louise! Ha ha!" This will make you very popular. You might even get invited to go behind a building for a Special Ceremony.

Also be sure to visit Carlsbad Caverns, an awesome geological formation in which visitors may witness the grandeur of more than 250 million bats. Do not startle them. The first atomic bomb was also built in New Mexico and is very slowly being restored to its original condition by workers with tweezers and extremely good eyesight.

New York

"The Empire State" is of course dominated by New York City, the "Big Apple," filled with the bustle and excitement of millions of energetic, sophisticated, urbane people experiencing numerous only-in-New-York thrills such as making it all the way to work without getting peed on. As Frank Sinatra put it in his immortal and dynamic rendering of New York's Official Horrendously Overexposed Hit Show Tune, "New York, New York":

> **If I can make it there,**
> **I can afford to move to Stamford,**
> **Connecticut.**

Here are some tips for getting maximum enjoyment from your trip to New York:

1. Cancel it immediately.

Ha ha! We are just kidding, of course. New York is in fact a major tourist destination, drawing millions of visitors each year, the majority of whom are never robbed and stabbed and left on the sidewalk to bleed to death while being stepped over by enough people to populate the entire state of Montana. Their secret? They follow certain common-sense New York City safety rules, such as:

- Always walk at least 30 miles per hour.
- Always keep your money and other valuables in a safe place, such as Switzerland.
- Avoid unsafe areas, such as your hotel bathroom.
- Never make eye contact. This is *asking* to be mugged. In the New York court system, a mugger is automatically declared not guilty if the defense can prove that the victim has a history of making eye contact.

Getting around New York is easy, thanks to the convenient and simple subway system. The major lines are the IRT, the BMT, the SAT, the LSD, and QED, which operate crosstown, midtown, downtown, thrutown, and camptown trains that are local and quasi-express only with alternating stations northbound between 59th Street and the corner of Twelfth Avenue and Grant's Tomb *only* on Wednesdays except during lobster season *or* for those passengers holding odd-numbered transfers and claiming more than 8.5 percent of their gross net deductible pretax noninterest income as medical expenses. If you have any questions about this, helpful attendants inside bullet-proof bomb-proof flame-proof machete-proof token-dispensing bunkers will be more than happy to continue reading the New York *Post*[7] no matter how loud you yell. Or for equal convenience you can take a taxi, which you get by simply raising your hand and then bringing it down sharply on the heads of the various New Yorkers who will try to leap into the taxi ahead of you. Be sure to speak very clearly to the driver, as he probably just arrived from a Third World nation where the major form of transportation is vines. The standard tip for everything in New York City is a smile and a bright, shiny quarter.

New York State is completely different.

North Carolina and Dakota

These two dynamic states are usually grouped together because they both begin with "North." The major products of North Carolina are tobacco and enormous amounts of phlegm. North Carolina also contains the famous "Lost Colony"; ask anyone for directions. North Dakota offers a fascinating array of wheat; the least-crowded time to visit is February.

[7]Headline: NAB PORN MOM IN TOT SLASH

Ohio

Ohio proudly calls itself "The Buckeye State," after the buckeye, a dynamic, hairless carnivorous nocturnal rodent that traps its prey by pretending to offer really good discounts on jewelry. The largest city in Ohio is Cleveland, which, after years of being the butt of many jokes, has risen to assume its rightful role among major American urban areas as the Future Home of the Rock and Roll Hall of Fame. We personally visited this attraction, which consisted of an office containing numerous press releases and a model of what the Hall of Fame would look like if it ever got built. The model is about the size of a harmonica. We think it would be a shrewd move on Cleveland's part to keep it on this scale, rather than building a full-size Hall of Fame, which would probably attract a lot of rowdy people going "WHOOO!" and throwing up on each other. Also, unlike a large building, the model can easily be placed in a briefcase and carried around the country for special events, parties, etc. ("Hey! Somebody sat on the Rock and Roll Hall of Fame!").

Other major Ohio cities include Akron ("The Rubber Capital of the World") and nearby Canton ("The Spermicidal Lubricant Capital of the World"). Ohio's Official State Literary Device is the metaphor.

Oklahoma

The frontier spirit of this dynamic state is best summed up by the Official State Song, from the

Rodgers and Hammerstein musical *Oklahoma*, which begins:

**Oooo-klahoma
If I can MAKE it there, I'll make it AN-y-where!**

This feeling dates back to the famous Oklahoma land rush of the 1880s, when the government opened Oklahoma for settlement and many would-be settlers came in "sooner" than they were supposed to, thereby earning the Oklahoma its proud nickname, "The Nutmeg State." Modern Oklahoma boasts both plant and animal life as well as the National Softball Hall of Fame, where every day from nine A.M. until six P.M. visitors may get into bitter, sometimes violent arguments over basically nothing. Oklahoma's Official State Mystery Food Additive is Sodium Erythorbate.

Oregon

Oregon is called "The Beaver State," although the University of Oregon team nickname is the "Ducks," which led to the following actual headline in the Seattle *Times* when an Oregon women's team lost to a team from the University of Washington (the "Huskies"):

HUSKY WOMEN SUBDUE DUCKS

The major industry in Oregon is trying to locate a tree that does not have an ecologist wrapped around it and then cutting it down and selling it to Japan to be converted into price stickers and pasted onto car windows for sale in the United States. Interesting Oregon sights include salmon, which every year return from the Pacific Ocean to swim up rivers, battling fierce currents, waterfalls, and hungry predators, until finally the survivors reach their spawning area, where, driven by an eons-old instinct, they realize that they forgot to bring the eggs.

Pennsylvania

Pennsylvania is a very historical state, especially Philadelphia, where on July 4, 1776, the Founding Fathers, defying the King and risking execution as traitors, held the Boston Massacre. Visitors to Philadelphia may see the famous Liberty Bell, which was built in 1776 for the fledgling American republic by the National Aeronautics and Space Administration, but which never really rang right because of a crack. Other popular Pennsylvania attractions include Pennsylvania Dutch Country, where visitors may see authentic tourists eating and looking around for Amish people to stare at; and Hershey, home of the world-famous Acne Hall of Fame. Pennsylvania's Official State Salad Dressing is ranch.

Rhode Island

Although it is the smallest state in the union, Rhode Island is nevertheless one of the least interesting.

Ha ha! We are just joshing, of course. This dynamic state is a vacation paradise, boasting a population, an average annual rainfall, and historical significance. For example, the Quonset hut was invented here. The Official State Bird (we are not making this up) is a chicken.

South Carolina and Dakota

Living up to their proud nickname, "The States Whose Names Begin With 'South,' " these two states offer an endless variety of dynamic places to visit, the most popular one being the Parris Island Marine Corps Recruit Depot, where visitors are welcome to lie facedown in the mud for six weeks while being yelled at by men with no foreheads. A major historic site is Fort Sumter, where in 1861 Confederate troops fired the fateful shots that struck Mount Rushmore, causing the formation of giant rock formations shaped like George Washington, Abraham Lincoln, Theodore Roosevelt, and Roger Maris. Also do NOT miss the spectacular Corn Palace in Mitchell, South Dakota, which is redecorated each fall with giant murals made from corn, expressing the theme: "We are going out of our *minds* up here."

Tennessee

Although Tennessee is what geographers call "a long, skinny state," it was nevertheless able for many years to contain Elvis Presley, whose Memphis home, Graceland, draws millions of visitors to marvel at The King's awesome legacy in the field of interior decoration, including a large room with a color scheme based entirely on digestive enzymes. Music lovers will also want to make a "beeline" for Nashville, home of the Grand Old Opera, which stages works by Wagner, Verdi, and Johnny Paycheck ("Take This Ring Trilogy and Shove It"). Tennessee also contains the Oak Ridge nuclear facility, where a 1957 laboratory mishap resulted in the Great Smoking Mountains. There are many other dynamic points of interest you'll want to see, but be on the lookout for the Tennessee Valley Authority, which is a very large man named Earl M. Potash, Jr. Do exactly what he says.

Texas

Texas used to be the largest state, but because of Alaska, it no longer is. Texans are still very touchy about this, so you should be sensitive when you discuss it with them. "What a large state this is, despite being nowhere NEAR as large as Alaska!" is a sensitive remark you might want to make. Although today Texas is modern and, of course, dynamic, it is proud of its cowboy tradition, which can still be seen in the form of men wearing comical hats. One of the most important historical attractions is the Alamo, the famous San Antonio mission where, in 1836, a small, brave band of Texans formed the nation's first car-rental franchise, which can still be seen today. Visitors are also welcome to the Lyndon B. Johnson Library, but they avoid it anyway. Texas also contains many scenic hills and rivers, although nothing like what you see in Alaska.[8] The Official State Symptom is irregularity.

Utah

Utah ("The Party State") draws millions of fun-lovers every year to such dynamic attractions such as the Great Salt Lake, where visitors may experience the excitement of getting salt all over themselves, followed by the excitement of trying to wash it off. They may *not*, however, put it in their foods, as seasonings are prohibited by law in Utah, along with alcohol, cigarettes, liquor, coffee, tea, and breath mints. Cocaine, on the other hand, is distributed free. The Official State Theoretical Particle is the quark.

Vermont

(See "New Hampshire.")

Virginia

When we think about all the history that has occurred in Virginia, we become so overwhelmed that we have to lie down on the sofa and yell for somebody to bring us a cold beer. Virginia was the site of North America's first permanent English colonist, James Town, as well as the first House of Burgesses, which was a house where they kept female burges. Tobacco was invented in Virginia, as well as George Washington

[8]Which is much larger than Texas

and seven other U.S. presidents: Jefferson, Monroe, Jefferson, Madison, Park, Lexington, and Third Avenue. The Civil War also occurred in Virginia in a number of national parks. Visitors may witness authentic demonstrations of all of these events, as well as a reenactment of the discovery of the radial tire, at Colonial Williamsburg, where each day men and women wearing authentic eighteenth-century costumes attempt to scratch themselves without anybody noticing. "Dynamic" is a word we would like to include in this sentence.

Washington

Washington is nicknamed "The Evergreen State" because it sounds better than "The Incessant Nagging Drizzle State." The largest city, Seattle, is one of the nation's most dynamic and fast-growing urban areas, with thousands of people arriving each week to enjoy a lifestyle that includes an abundant natural supply of slugs. Mount Rainier, an extraordinarily beautiful volcanic peak some fifty miles from the city, blew up in 1963, but nobody in Seattle is aware of this yet because the weather has been pretty cloudy. Seattle also features a giant Space Needle, which is connected via a monorail to a giant Space Catheter. Washington's Official State Battery Size is AAA.

Washington, D.C.

As an American, you owe it to yourself to visit the nation's capital, because this is *your* city, where *your* government spends trillions of *your* dollars on dynamic programs such as National Intestinal Blockage Month, administered by *your* government workers in buildings that *you* can't go into because *you* don't have a pass. But you can visit many inspirational tourist sites, including the Richard M. Nixon Monument (currently missing) and the Tomb of the Unknown Internal Revenue Service Employee Who Is Supposed to Answer the Taxpayer Assistance Hot Line. You may also visit the White House any time, day or night, simply by pounding on the front gate and shouting vague irrational threats. Another popular Washington stop is the Supreme Court, where the justices frequently ask the spectators to help them decide a tough case by registering their opinions on the Applause-O-Meter. And be sure to visit your congressperson's office, where you are welcome to take some souvenir furniture. Your congressperson probably won't notice. Your congressperson is probably in Paris.

West Virginia

The appeal of this dynamic, rugged state is perhaps best described by the words of mega-weenie John Denver, who sang:

Almost heaven? *West Virginia?*

West Virginia has long been a major attraction for tourists who seeking to escape from their "nine-to-five" office-bound jobs for a chance to get out in the country and mine some coal. West Virginia's residents are all very friendly and closely related. You can meet them "up close and personal" during the state's annual Deliverance Canoe Trip and Pig Imitation Festival. West Virginia's Official State Toilet Part is the flapper.

Wisconsin

Wisconsin ("The Moo State") is of course best known for being highly cow-intensive, but this state has *much* more to offer the visitor, as is shown by the following actual quotation from the Wisconsin article in *World Book Encyclopedia*: "The state is a leader in canning peas." There is little that we can add to describe the raw excitement of this dynamic state, except to say that (1) the malted milk was invented in Wisconsin in 1887, and (2) a Wisconsin store once sold us a rubber hat shaped like a giant wedge of cheese, and quite frankly, when we were wearing that hat we could have had any woman we wanted.[9] Wisconsin's Official State Interjection is "Huh."

Wyoming

Wyoming—often called "The Very Last State That We Have to Write About in This Chapter, Thank God"—contains a great deal of scenery such as the Grand Tetons, which get their name from the Indian expression, "Get a load of those Tetons." The major

[9]Not that we ever did

attraction is Yellowstone National Park, where nature-loving visitors may learn about the wilderness by witnessing as federal bears, acting on instinct, rummage through Dodge minivans, tossing tourists aside in their quest for Hostess Twinkies. Yellowstone also features Old Faithful Geyser, an amazing natural phenomenon that, at regularly scheduled intervals, erupts out of the ground and performs "Hello Dolly." Tips are appreciated.

OTHER COUNTRIES BESIDES US IN THE WESTERN HEMISPHERE (Yes! There ARE Some!)

You don't have to go all the way to Europe to be in a foreign country, because there are several nice ones right here in our own continent.[10] Among the numerous cultural advantages of visiting these countries are the following:

1. They are nearby.
2. They get American TV.

The largest of our North American neighbors are, of course, Canada and Mexico, both of which share lengthy borders with the United States, and both of which have long maintained peaceful relations with us based on mutual trust and respect and a heartfelt understanding of the fact that any time we feel like

---

[10]North America

it we can nuke them into radioactive grit. Let's take a closer look at these two "friendly neighbors" and see if we can't learn to appreciate them more without picking up any actual information.

CANADA

Although we hardly ever think about it except when the TV weather person is showing us a cold air mass, Canada is actually a major country, with an area of more than 169 billion hectometers in longitude, and a bustling population of more than 27 million, if you include members of the wolverine family. There are also a number of humans living up there, and in many ways they have a lifestyle quite similar to ours, including such traditional American activities as driving Japanese cars. The major difference is that Canada is divided into two major linguistic groups— English speakers and French speakers—which have learned, over the course of 300 years of cohabitation, to hate each other. The result is that everything in Canada has to be written in both English and French, which creates a hazardous situation because the two languages frequently disagree, as we can see from these actual Canadian signs:

STOP

ALLEZ[11]

[11]"Go"

NO SPITTING!

**HAWKEZ-VOUS UNE GRANDE GOBBE
TOUTE DE SUITE!**[12]

Despite these differences, Canada has developed into an actual nation with cities, an economy, comical-looking money with beavers on it, etc. To understand how this happened, we need to review:

The History of Canada

Canadian history began 20,000 years ago when primitive people came across the land bridge from Asia to watch the quarter-finals of the National Hockey League playoffs, which are still going on. Then nothing happened until 1497, when King Henry VII of England hired an Italian explorer named John Cabot to try to reach Asia by—those explorers were always trying wacky stunts like this—sailing across the Atlantic. Instead, Cabot—he could easily have avoided this by the simple precaution of looking at a map—wound up in Canada. Here is an actual quotation about this event from the *World Book Encyclopedia*:

> Cabot found no such luxuries as jewels or spices. But he saw an enormous amount of cod.

[12]"Emit A Big Lunger Right Now!"

Whoo! I bet THAT thrilled old Henry VII, don't you? Picture the scene: he's sitting on his throne, all excited because he's been waiting for months and months, and he can hardly wait to see what kinds of jewels he's going to get for his investment, and Cabot hands him a bag of dead cod and says: "And there's plenty more where THAT came from!"

From that day forward Canada was considered to be very desirable, and eventually the British and French got into a big rivalry over it, which resulted in a series of wars called "The Series of Wars Between the British and the French." This dispute was finally settled in 1763 when the British forces defeated the French in the Battle of Kicking Some French Butt, after which the two sides signed the Treaty of the Two Sides, under which Britain got to keep Canada, and France got to visit for three weeks during the summer.

After that Canada continued to grow and have many important historical events, among which, according to the *World Book Encyclopedia*, were: Growing Discontent, Lord Durham's Report, The Return of MacDonald, and Foreign Relations. Also at some point a government formed. The Canadian government consists of a prime minister, whose primary function is to meet with the U.S. president once a year and ask in a whiny voice how come we keep dropping acid rain on them. The president always replies that we'll stop the acid rain if they'll stop the cold air masses. Then the two leaders share a hearty laugh and shake hands, because they know that we're really close international friends. Plus we still have the nukes.

What to See in Canada

Canada boasts numerous **goose-infested lakes** and several **major cities** that rival New York for **sophistication**, defined as **lack of parking**. There is also a **Vast Arctic Wasteland** where visitors are welcome to come and get **lost** and try to survive by eating their own **parka linings**. The Vast Arctic Wasteland is one of Canada's **ten provinces**, the other ones being Toronto, Greenland, Quahog, Alberto, Pierre, Roberta, North Dakota, Manitoba,[13] and the Yucatan. All of these provinces feature **culture** as well as **hydroelectric power**, and are well worth a visit. But the Canadian tourist attraction that we rank highest of all, despite the fact that we have not technically been there in person, is the **Head-Smashed-In Buffalo Jump**. We are not making this attraction up. It's an **extremely historical site** where, many years ago, **Native American tribespersons** used to kill **buffalo** by driving them off the edge of a **cliff**. According to the legend, one day a tribesperson decided to watch this event from under the cliff, and numerous buffalo landed on his **head**, which, as you are well aware, is generally fatal, and thus the site got its name: Total Moron Cliff. No, **seriously**, it really is called the Head-Smashed-In Buffalo Jump, and the Canadian government has set up an **interpretive centre** there, and when we called it up, a person answered the phone as follows: "Head Smashed In, may I help you?" This was probably the **highlight of our entire life**.

---

[13]Literally, "Many Tubas"

🚶🚶 CANADA FACTS AT A GLANCE

Spelling of "Center"—Incorrect
Beavers on Currency—Yes
Hockey Players with Teeth—No

MEXICO

The first thing you have to understand, as a visitor to Mexico, is that you do not, automatically, the instant you arrive, develop a fierce case of the trots. That's an unfounded myth that epitomizes the condescending attitude that many North Americans have toward Mexico, and we'd like to shatter it right here and now. We have personally visited Mexico, and we found it to be a charming and hospitable place filled with exciting things to do, although unfortunately our activities were somewhat limited by the fact that the instant we arrived we developed a fierce case of the trots. But we definitely enjoyed what we saw, and we made it our business to see every single important historic and cultural site in the entire nation that was within a two-minute sprint of our hotel bathroom. These sites included the **hotel bar**, the **hotel restaurant**, the **hotel gift shop**, and the **hotel hallway leading back to our bathroom**, all of which revealed the rich cultural tapestry that Mexico possesses due to all the history that has occurred there in the past.

The History of Mexico

The history of Mexico dates back thousands of years to the time of the Indians, who, of course, were not aware that they were Indians because nobody from Europe had discovered them yet. Despite this handicap, they had developed a great civilization featuring many advanced concepts including mathematics, writing, architecture, a highly advanced calendar,[14] and an alarm clock with the "snooze" feature. These Indians built numerous ruins that can still be seen today,[15] as well as a number of major pyramids, which were made by lifting enormous stones and which served as monuments to Xinzthiznclxn, the God of Hernias. Then, in the sixteenth century, the Spanish showed up and introduced Western civilization until just about everybody was dead. This was followed, in order, by the seventeenth, eighteenth, and nineteenth centuries, during which Mexico included a large section of what is now the United States, including Texas, California, Hawaii, and Rhode Island. Mexico graciously yielded these lands to the United States in 1848 under the Treaty of Sign This Treaty or We Blow Your Head Off. Eventually there was a revolution, starring Seymour A. "Pancho" Villa, a heroic figure who rode around having exciting adventures with his comical sidekick and carving his initials into people's shirts with his sword. Or maybe that was Zorro. But in any event, there was finally a revolution, and today Mexico is a modern happy nation of 90 million people, 87 million of whom currently reside in Los Angeles.

[14]For example, it had Lincoln's birthday
[15]Thursday

What to Do in Mexico

Well for one thing, there is a tremendous amount of **Mexican food**, which is **delicious** and **perfectly safe** as long as you are careful never to get any of it in your **digestive system**. You will want to visit the ancient cities of **Quzxnclznaontxnzl, Czqnxzlnqlnxz** and **Zxqcnxcxnzxclqnxlnzqnlnxn**, which offer **thought-provoking, fact-filled lectures** by **leading cultural anthropologists**, followed by **live human sacrifices**.[16] Also, you may want to attend a **bullfight**, although you must be careful never to **stand up**, because that's how you indicate that you wish to participate in the **Amateur Matador Event**.

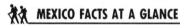

MEXICO FACTS AT A GLANCE

Unit of Currency—The Lambada
Loose Chickens—Yes

---

[16]Check local listings

Traveling in Europe

(''EXCUSE ME! WHERE IS THE *BIG* MONA LISA?'')

As a traveler, you will eventually want to broaden your cultural horizons by visiting the Home of Western Civilization, the source of many of the values and ideals that we cherish so deeply today, the birthplace of our culture: Yankee Stadium. But if you get a chance, you should also visit Europe.

A BRIEF HISTORY OF EUROPE

Although from outer space Europe appears to be shaped like a large ketchup stain, it actually consists of a many small separate nations, each with a proud and ancient tradition of hating all the other ones.

The first European was a Cro-Magnon man who wandered around for about 65,000 years looking for food, only to discover that everything was closed (this is still true today). So he was hungry and lonely, which led to the invention of agriculture and, later, the discotheque.

Meanwhile, in Greece, civilization was forming. The Greeks, aided by a warm climate, had invented geometry, and they used this advanced knowledge to conquer the surrounding cultures by piercing them with the ends of isosceles triangles. This led to the Golden Age of Greece, which was marked by the spread of restaurants to outposts as far away as Brooklyn, parts of which can still be seen today.

Eventually Greece was conquered by Alexander the Great of Macedonia with the aid of a new weapon, the rhomboid. Alexander ruled his empire until somebody did some checking and discovered that there was no such place as "Macedonia," which paved the way for the Roman Empire. The Romans spent the next 200 years using their great engineering skill to construct ruins all over Europe. The basic Roman ruin design is a pile of rocks with a little plaque saying "Roman Ruins" and a group of tourists frowning at it and wishing they were back at the hotel bar.

At this point Europe was invaded by barbarian motorcycle gangs such as the Angles, the Franks, the Jutes, the Teds, the Sextants, the Ventricles, and Martha and the Vandellas. This led to the Middle Ages, which were characterized by strict zoning regulations requiring that every 250 yards there had to be a giant cathedral built from stones the size of Raymond Burr. This made life extremely difficult for the laborers—many of whom had never even *heard* of Raymond Burr—so everybody was very happy when the Renaissance broke out in the fourteenth century at about 2:30 P.M.

The Renaissance was a time of cultural rebirth during which everybody lost a few pounds and started taking night courses. There were many scientific and technological advances such as the plow, the stapler, and, above all, the printing press, which enabled mass production of the first popular work of literature, a novel called *Hot Moist Serfs*:

"𝕻riscilla," said 𝕭art, unable to restrain his passion any longer. "𝕴 want you right now, right here, in the barley field."

𝕻riscilla blushed, but she was secretly pleased, for she could not help but notice that 𝕭art had a very large plow.

The Renaissance collapsed from exhaustion in 1600, after which everybody rested up in preparation for the Era of a Whole Bunch of Wars, which included the Franco-Prussian War; the Franco-Anglo-Russo War, the Hundred Years War, the Franco-Austro-Russo-Hungro War, The Nine Years War, The Frank O'Brien War, The 36 Months or 50,000 Miles Whichever Comes First War, The War of the Tuna Casseroles, and Super Bowl XVIII. All this conflict caused Europe to gradually disintegrate, so that today it contains many tiny nations, with names like

"Lichtenburg," that could not hold their own, militarily, against the UCLA Pep Squad. The tragic result is that modern-day European nations have had to content themselves with developing sound economies, while the United States, as a Major World Power, has enjoyed the privilege of getting its butt shot at all over the world.

Nevertheless there are still many exciting things to see and do in Europe, although you, personally, will not get to see and do them, because you'll be too busy frowning at Roman ruins. The best way to locate these is to be on a large guided bus tour. You want the kind that stops at everything in Europe for fifteen minutes, which is just enough time to get off the bus, take a picture of whatever it is, and get back on the bus, unless you have to go to the bathroom, in which case you have time to get off the bus, pee on whatever it is, and get back on the bus. There are many other advantages to being with a large tour group, such as:

1. It gives you an excellent opportunity to get to know the other couples in the tour group, which is a broadening cultural experience because some of them will come from completely different states. You'll end up exchanging Christmas cards with them for years and years, and when you die, your spouse will write them a little note, and they'll say: "Remember so-and-so? From New Jersey? The one we met on the tour? The one with the big hat? In the plumbing-supplies business? Well, he died."

2. In addition to meeting people on your tour group, you will encounter people from new and completely *different* tour groups, because you will all be stopping at the same popular attractions, which have been thoughtfully preselected for you based on their cultural interest as measured in square footage of parking area.

3. Many tours give everybody a complimentary plastic flight bag with the official tour logo printed on it, which you all carry at all times so you can instantly identify other members of your tour. This is very important when you are in an emergency foreign situation such as, for example, the Louvre Museum in Paris, France, and you need to make an observation such as: "You call that the Mona Lisa? Back home we got illustrated dish towels bigger than that!"

4. Being on a tour is the only way you can be guaranteed of seeing every cathedral in Europe. If you were traveling alone, once you realized that all cathedrals are basically large dark buildings that smell like unwashed gym shorts, you might, in a weak moment, be tempted to skip one or two. But this is not possible on a tour. No sir. Your bus will stop at every single one. In fact, many travel experts recommend that you take a piece of chalk and place a distinctive mark on each cathedral you visit, because sometimes the tour guides, as a prank, will take a group to the same one five or six times in a single afternoon.

Wherever you go on your tour, be sure to take hundreds of color photographs, so that when you get home you can invite your friends and neighbors over for an educational presentation wherein you say, "Okay, now this is one of Bernice standing in front of this cathedral in Bologne, which is in Germany. Or Norway." And Bernice can say: "No, that cathedral is in England, because I remember I wore my beige pumps in England, because my maroon pumps gave me this awful blister, which finally popped in Notre Dame, which is a cathedral in . . . Hey! Where's everybody going? There's more pictures!"

PASSPORT

To enter Europe, you must have a valid passport with a photograph of yourself in which you look like you are being booked on charges of soliciting sheep. To obtain your passport, you must wait in a federal waiting room with yellow walls for a minimum of two hours, then produce proof of U.S. citizenship in the form of a personal letter from Publishers Clearing House notifying you that you have probably won a million dollars.

MEDICAL CARE IN EUROPE

Medical care in Europe is excellent, and you may rest assured that if God forbid anything were to happen to you, the hospital personnel will use only the highest-quality stainless-steel drill to bore a hole in your skull to let out the Evil Spirits.

Ha ha! We are just joshing, of course. There is really nothing at all primitive about European medical care except that in some countries they practice it in foreign languages, meaning you run the risk of entering the hospital complaining of an inflamed appendix and coming out as a member of a completely different gender. This is why many smart travelers take the precaution of having the international symbol for "No Sex-Change Operation, Thank You"[1] tattooed on or near their private parts. It's also a good idea to take along any prescription medication that you might need, as well as a spare pair of eyeglasses, some clean bandages, sutures, a scalpel, a wheelchair, and a CAT-scan machine. Feel free to drink the water in Europe, but don't touch the food.

CUSTOMS

Before they let you into Europe, you have to pass through Customs, so that beady-eyed individuals can root freely through your underwear looking for certain items that are strictly prohibited in Europe, such as cold drinks and functional toilet paper. European toilet paper is made from the same material that Americans use for roofing, which is why Europeans tend to remain standing throughout soccer matches.

---

[1] A circle with a line through it superimposed over a pair of pruning shears

Helpful Hints for Getting Through Customs

Narcotics: You are not allowed to bring narcotics into Europe, and you are *definitely* not allowed to sell them to children. It's a good idea to assure the customs personnel that you are aware of these rules. Try to bring the subject up in a casual manner. "So!" you could say. "Nice weather we're having here in Europe! By the way, I'm not bringing in any narcotics, and I certainly don't intend to sell them to children!"

Insects: The Europeans do not want you bringing in insects that will reproduce like crazy and eat all their agriculture. Any insects you bring in must be spayed, and you should be prepared to prove it to the customs officials. "Go ahead!" you should tell them in a challenging manner. "Just try to arouse this insect!"

Tipping: Remember that the customs personnel are working men and women just like everybody else, and they definitely appreciate receiving "a little something" in return for a job well done. Your best approach is to hand them a shiny quarter right up front, then, with a wink and a friendly smile, tell them, "Do a good job with these bags, and there'll be another one of these for each of you!"

MEASUREMENTS IN EUROPE

Europe operates under the metric, or communist, system of measurement. The main units are the kilometer, the hectare, the thermometer, the pfennig, the libra, the megawatt, and the epigram. These are all very easy to remember because all you have to do is divide them by a specific number, possibly 100. Or you can use the following handy conversion table:

Metric System		Real System
One Kilometer	equals	about five miles
Five Kilometers	equals	about five miles
Ten Kilometers	equals	about five miles
Eight Pentagrams ...	equals	about five miles
1830 Hours	equals	about eight days

DRIVING IN EUROPE

Europeans, like some Americans, drive on the right side of the road, except in England, where they drive on *both* sides of the road; Italy, where they drive on the sidewalk; and France, where if necessary they will follow you right into the hotel lobby. If you have a valid U.S. driver's license, you may drive in most European countries, but it's more efficient to simply leap off a cliff.

CHANGING MONEY

Aside from not comprehending menus, changing money is the most popular activity for Americans in Europe. There are money-changing booths every-where, occupied by little men crouching inside next to incomprehensible signs covered with numbers and letters like this:

UAR 23.402490029
UAW @3049.5858, 2 FOR 43-0394-02342
USA 349239%92182
UCLA 37 USC 14 3rd quarter

These numbers change constantly to reflect the fact that the dollar is getting weaker. The first rule of travel finance is that no matter what is going on elsewhere in the world, the dollar is always getting weaker where *you* are. By the time you've spent a couple of days in a foreign country, the natives will be blowing their noses on the dollar. To change your money, simply give the little man enough dollars to buy a decent used car. He will perform various calculations involving the exchange rate and the Dow Jones Industrial Average and the relative humidity, then thrust out an amount of foreign currency so small that if you threw it into a fountain for good luck, you would immediately be struck by lightning. You should repeat this process after every meal.

HOW TO USE A BIDET

One of the things you'll need to get used to in Europe is the bidet, which is a bathroom appliance, usually located next to the toilet, that looks like a urinal lying on its back. If you want the Europeans to think that you're a suave and sophisticated person, as opposed to the nose-picking yahoo that you actually are, you need to learn proper bidet procedure. The number one rule is:

1. Never pee in the bidet.

This is *extremely* important. This is how the Europeans separate the sheep from the goats, sophisticationwise. In fact, it's a good idea, when you emerge from a European bathroom, to state in a loud yet casual voice, "Well, *I* sure didn't pee in the bidet, ha ha!"

So the question is, what *are* you supposed to do with a bidet? The answer is: *wash your private parts*. Really. Now I know what you're thinking, as an American. You're thinking: Wait a minute! Don't they wash their private parts in the *shower*? The shocking answer is: no. Studies show that Europeans hardly ever even *take* showers. Highly sophisticated European cultures such as the French also wear the same underwear several days in a row, to the point where individual jockey shorts, when they are finally removed for laundering, have to be subdued with hammers. Thus you can easily see the need for some kind of major hygiene unit in the European bathroom, although you yourself, as an unsophisticated shower-taking American, don't need to bother with it. But to avoid offending your European hosts, you should at least *pretend* that you used it when you emerge from the bathroom. "Boy!" you should say. "My private parts are clean as a whistle!" ("Garçon! Mes partes de privatude sont net comme un sifflet!")

SPECIFIC NATIONS IN EUROPE

As we mentioned earlier, Europe is actually made up of specific nations. Although most of them belong to the European Economic Community (NATO)—a multinational organization that administers tariffs, trade, bowling banquets, etc.—each nation has its own customs, traditions, and hand gestures. So the remainder of this chapter will be devoted to a country-by-country breakdown, including helpful tips and points of interest. Although we have made every effort to ensure that this information is both timely and accurate, please bear in mind that (1) conditions are subject to change, and (2) we are a big fat liar.

Austria

Austria is a very wonderful country that we have fond memories of despite the fact that, when we went there, virtually every single person we dealt with tried to shortchange us. We're sure that this was just a fluke, and we are certainly not going to dwell, in this fair and unbiased travel book, upon the fact that *virtually every single person we dealt with in Austria tried to shortchange us.* "Let bygones be bygones," is our motto. Also several times people yelled at us for jaywalking. This will happen to you, in the stricter nations. People over there haven't had a chance to develop an appreciation for American-style democracy, where it says right in the *Constitution* that you can jaywalk. But aside from the strictness and the

CONSTANT SHORTCHANGING

we found Austria to be a really wonderful place, really, even if they did accuse us, in a particularly nasty manner, of not having paid the rental-car deposit, and then, after a lengthy argument in which it finally became clear that we *had* paid it, they did not apologize at all, but in fact got even *nastier*, not that this is important, any more than the

SHORTCHANGING EPIDEMIC

that appeared to be sweeping the nation when we were there. Because the truth is that Austria has many really wonderful attractions, which unfortunately because of space constraints we are unable to list here.

🚶 AUSTRIA FACTS AT A GLANCE

Currency Unit: The Pflugenhaffenlepzeigenhohenzollern (or "Winkie")
Language: Foreign
Tipping: Not Permitted
Littering Punishable By: Death
Alps: Yes
Taco Bells: No

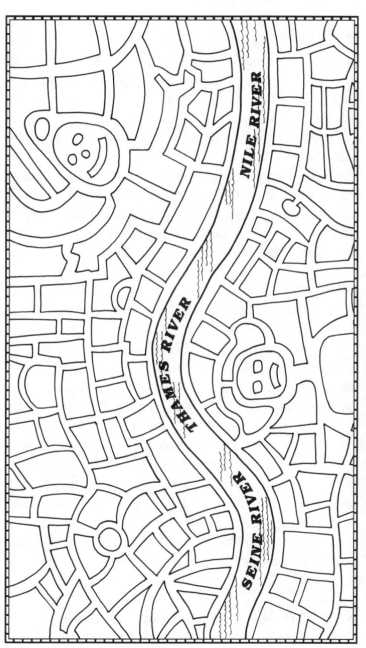

MAP OF DOWNTOWN VIENNA

Belgium

Belgium is a small nation containing people who call themselves—this is true—"Walloons." They are not ashamed of this at all. "I myself am a Walloon" is the kind of thing they say all the time. It's called "Walloon Pride." Belgium also contains people who call themselves "Flemings," although fortunately there is no actual place called "Flem." The result of this fascinating cultural mix is that Belgium has a number of official languages, including French, Dutch, German, Italian, Spanish, Greek, Latin, Cajun, Moldavian, and Frantic Arm Gestures.

HISTORY: Because of poor planning on the part of its first king, Roger XVIXMN (1606–present), Belgium was originally located between Germany and France, which for several centuries declared war on each other as often as modern nations declare things like Cheese Appreciation Month. The result was that Belgium became what historians call "The Screen Door of Europe," constantly getting slammed as various armies went racing through in both directions, often failing to wipe their feet. In the modern era this problem has been solved by moving Belgium to a safer location, up near the Netherlands, Denmark, Luxembourg, Iceland, and Canada, which are known collectively as "The Weenie Nations," so it's perfectly safe now. Although we ourselves would take a gas mask.

WHAT TO SEE IN BELGIUM: They have a *bunch* of buildings.

WHEN TO GO: This Wednesday would be good. But *not* next Monday, because Belgium has a dental appointment. It is also closed during the festival of the Six Kinds of Mustard.

🚶🚶 BELGIUM FACTS AT A GLANCE

　　Currency Unit: The Pfarthing
　　Height: Average
　　Motto: Dieu et Droit Pour La Vérité ("I Spit
　　　On Your Zither")
　　Favorite Song: "Mustang Sally"

Bulgaria

There's always plenty to see and do in Bulgaria!

Denmark

Denmark (also called "Norway") is best known as the original home of the prune Danish as well as the Vikings, who wore hats with horns sticking out of them, and for a very good reason: they were insane. But this did not stop them from being bold mariners who actually reached North America before Columbus did, although they were stripped of the title when blood tests revealed that they had used steroids.

Modern-day Denmark is a tourism wonderland, boasting a year-round average temperature of 14 degrees Centipede (108 degrees Richter). The most famous city is Copenhagen, where Hans Christian

Andersen wrote such pioneering children's classics as *Horton Hears a Whom* and *The Ugly Teenaged Mutant Ninja Duckling*. While in Copenhagen you simply *must* take a stroll down Bjarnkvaalastraa-denjkrn, taking a left on Kveljnorlagnarbenkanklen, then your first right onto Hralgnekjarnklenvaagen-dam. Go up to a man wearing a green overcoat and tell him: "The oyster owns a fine wristwatch." He will know what to do.

🚶🚶 DENMARK FACTS AT A GLANCE

Language: Swedish

Currency Unit: The Rune (12 Runes = 1 Kvetch)

National Anthem: "Vie Aar Knut Hebben Nu Longkenflukn"

("We Are Not Having Any Lung Flukes")

England

England is one of four nations, along with Ireland, Scotland, and New Zealand, that make up the British Isles. England is a very popular foreign country to visit because the people there speak some English. Usually, however, when they get to the crucial part of a sentence they'll use words that they made up, such as "scone" and "ironmonger." As a sophisticated traveler, you should learn some British words so you can avoid communications mixups, as is shown by these examples:

Example 1: The Unsophisticated Traveler
ENGLISH WAITER: May I help you?
TRAVELER: I'd like an inedible roll, please.
ENGLISH WAITER *(confused)*: Huh?
Example 2: The Sophisticated Traveler
ENGLISH WAITER: May I help you?
TRAVELER: I'd like an ironmonger, please.
ENGLISH WAITER: Coming right up!

Speaking of food, English cuisine has received a lot of unfair criticism over the years, but the truth is that it can be a very pleasant surprise to the connoisseur of severely overcooked livestock organs served in lukewarm puddles of congealed grease. England manufactures most of the world's airline food, as well as all the food you ever ate in your junior-high-school cafeteria. Some traditional English dishes are Toad in the Hole, Bubble and Squeak, Cock-a-Leekie Soup, Spotted Dick, Bug-in-a-Bucket, Willie One-Polyp, Tonsil-and-Toast, Whack-a-Doodle Johnson, and Fester Pudding. Attractive displays of these dishes—some of them dating back to the sixteenth century—can be found in bars called "pubs," where the English traditionally gather to drink, glance at the food, and continue drinking.

But the main attraction in England is history. You cannot throw a scone in England without hitting a hallowed ancient object such as the actual chair that King Ralph the Easily Amused sat in when he made peace with the Duke of Whomping in 1123. You should definitely visit as many of these historic sites as you can before you starve. Among the most important ones are:

The Tower of London: This is the home of the Crown Jewels, a collection of gem-encrusted swords, headwear, plates, and utensils such as the priceless Spatula of India, all guarded by the famous "Beefeaters." The Crown Jewels belong to the royal family, whose members tried for centuries to get them back, only to have their heads whacked off by the famous Beefeaters, which is why the royal family now uses paper plates.

Arizona Bridge: This was originally located in Arizona, but was moved to London as a tourist attraction in 1362 by King Eddreth the Big Fan of Onions.

Westminster Abbey: This is an extremely old building where many famous dead British people such as John Milton,[2] Rudyard Kipling, and Charlie Watts are buried in the floor. It's not clear why the British did this. The best we can figure is that it must have been raining very hard during the funerals, and somebody said, "What the hell, let's just bury them right here in the floor."

Buckingham Palace: This is, of course, the home of the famous British royal family, which upholds many ancient cherished British traditions such as the tradition of Wearing Comical Hats and the tradition of Appearing on the Cover

[2]Bass player for the Kinks

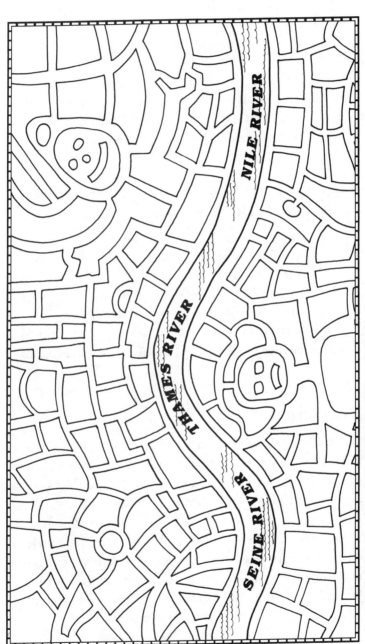

MAP OF DOWNTOWN LONDON

of *People* Magazine at Least Once Per Month ("Fergie: Does She Have Shingles?"). Each day thousands of tourists gather at the palace to watch the famous ceremony of the Changing of the Guard, which follows the ceremonies of the Bathing of the Guard and the Sprinkling of Some Talcum Powder on the Guard's Butt.

🚶🚶 ENGLAND FACTS AT A GLANCE

Unit of Currency: The Thruppence
   (2 Thruppence = 2 Bodkins)
Sign: Capricorn
Track: Wet
Queen's Wardrobe By: Mister Duane's House
   of Vision Impairment

Finland

Located partly inside the Arctic Circle, Finland has long been a popular destination with travelers who enjoy the feeling of knowing that if their car breaks down, they could be eaten by wolves. Finland is also the home of the sauna, which is a wooden box in which you subject your body to extreme heat, which causes you to become very relaxed, unless of course the door gets stuck, in which case it causes you to become lasagna. We ourselves prefer to stay outside and take our chances with the wolves.

The major city in Finland is Helsinki, home of the world-famous Gverjkinklankerwanker, or "Tower of Linoleum."

FINLAND FACTS AT A GLANCE

Unit of Currency: The Fermkin
Form of Government: A small but powerful
  woman named Helga
Brad: Oh, Marcia, I have missed you so!
Marcia: Oh, Brad, really?
  (*They embrace*)

France

First of all, let's dispense with this absurd stereotypical notion that the French are rude. The French are *not* rude. They just happen to hate *you*. But that is no reason to bypass this beautiful country, whose master chefs have a well-deserved worldwide reputation for trying to trick people into eating snails. Nobody is sure how this got started. Probably a couple of French master chefs were standing around one day, and they found a snail, and one of them said: "I bet that if we called this something like 'escargot,' tourists would eat it." Then they had a hearty laugh, because "escargot" is the French word for "fat crawling bag of phlegm."

This spirit of daring culinary innovation persists in France, which has also pioneered such advances as:

- The entree that costs as much as a set of radial tires and consists of a very large plate that appears at first to be totally empty except for a tiny speck of dirt that turns out, upon closer inspection, to be the entree. (A top French chef can carry an entire year's supply of entrees in his wallet.)
- The waiter who makes it extremely clear that he did not get into the waiter business to waste his valuable time actually *waiting on* people, especially not lowlife scum such as yourself who clearly would not know the difference between fine French cuisine and Cheez Whiz.
- The tip that is automatically included For Your Convenience even if your food arrives festooned with armpit hairs (les haires du pitte).

So you will definitely want to go to some fine French restaurants. We don't mean go *inside* them. We mean stand around outside with the other tourists staring incomprehendingly at the menu, which should look like this:

CARTE DE MENU
———

Les Petites Eyeballes de Mackerelle en Huile de Voiture
Le Debenture en Camisole au Bibliothèque
Le Spamme avec un Side de Fries
Le Poisson du Votre Frère Raoul
Le Roni du Zoo en La Ware de la Tupper

Prix Pour Le Wholle Ball de Waxe: 156,000,000,000,000,000 Francs

---

Le Financing Available

"Vouz Tried the Rest, Now Try Le Best"

Once you've looked at the menu for a while, it's time to enjoy a hearty one-ounce bag of peanuts saved from your plane trip over, then set out to view:

The Attractions of France

One of the main attractions is of course the world-famous **Eiffel Tower**, which created a lot of controversy when it was erected in 1889 because the builder, Alexandre Gustave Eiffel, had presold it as a condominium. "Where the hell are the walls?" the buyers wanted to know. "Where are we supposed to go to the bathroom?" This is still a problem at the tower, so don't stand too close.

Another well-known Paris landmark is the **Arc de Triomphe**, a moving monument to the many brave men and women who have died trying to visit it, which we do not recommend because it's located in the middle of La Place de la Traffic Coming from All Directions at 114 Miles Per Hour. But you should definitely visit the **Louvre**, a world-famous art museum where you can view, at close range, the backs of thousands of other tourists trying to see the **Mona Lisa**, which actually was stolen in 1978, but the crowd is so dense that it doesn't matter. People come away convinced that they've seen it, similar to the

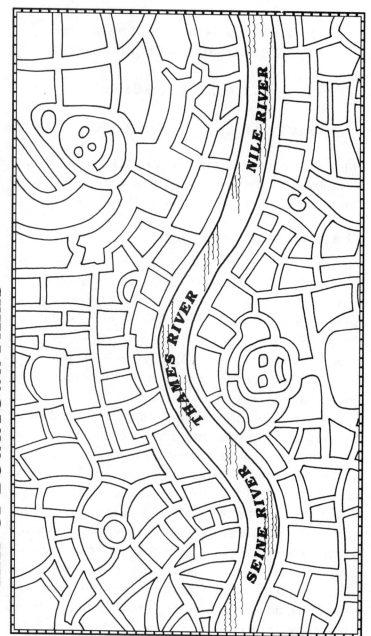

MAP OF DOWNTOWN PARIS

way people in underdeveloped nations are always seeing the face of Jesus on the skins of yams. Also in the Louvre are various **statues with pieces missing**; visitors are welcome to try to patch these up.

A Good Conversation-Starter in France:

"I guess you guys really bit the big one in World War Two, huh?"

 **FRANCE FACTS AT A GLANCE**

National Underwear Changing Day: March 12

Official Dance: The Gator

Germany

Germany is really a very nice nation that used to have an unfortunate tendency to fall in with the wrong crowd every few decades and try to take over the world. But that is all in the past, thank goodness. After years of painful division, East and West Germany are finally back together as a large, vibrant, strong, dynamic, extremely powerful and heavily armed nation that we are sure will be a Good Neighbor for . . . LOOK OUT! HERE THEY COME!!

Ha ha! We are just poking a little friendly fun at Germany, which is famous for enjoying a good joke, or as the Germans say, "Sprechnehaltenzoltenfussenmachschnitzerkalbenrollen." Here is just one hilarious example of what we are talking about:

FIRST GERMAN: How many Polish people does it take to screw in a light bulb?
SECOND GERMAN: I don't know! How many?
FIRST GERMAN: Let's invade Poland and find out!
MILLIONS OF OTHER GERMANS: Okay!

No! We're just kidding! Probably! The truth is that we like Germany a lot. In fact, we celebrated our fortieth birthday there with some friends, the idea being that if we were going to get old, we should do it while surrounded by the maximum possible quantity of beer. They have wonderful beer in Germany, and they serve it in containers so large that, in other nations, they would be used as shelters for the homeless. This gives new meaning to the concept of "having a beer." In the United States, "having a beer" is a semi-harmless act that leaves you feeling slightly mellow, whereas in Germany it can leave you dancing naked on the roof of a moving bus.[3]

Eating in Germany is easy, because there is basically only one kind of food, called the "wurst." This is a delicious item made by compressing random pig parts until they have reached the density of bowling balls, then serving them in long brown units that don't look at *all* like large bowel movements, so just put that thought right out of your mind. At first, all wursts seem the same, but in fact each region of the country has its own "special recipe," thus producing

[3]This requires a permit; ask your travel agent

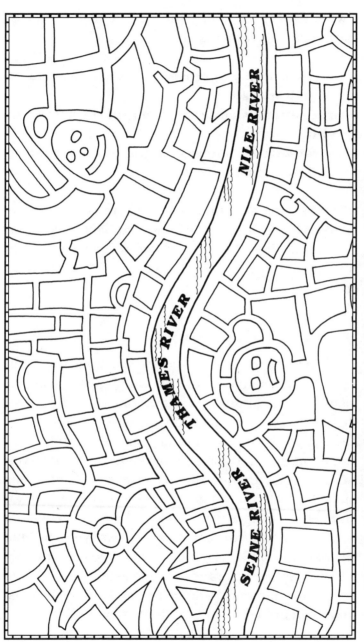

MAP OF DOWNTOWN BERLIN OR MUNICH

a wide variety for your eating excitement. Some of our personal favorites are:

Blattwurst: Compressed pig parts served in 7-inch units

Grosswurst: Compressed pig parts served in 8-inch units

Wurstwurst: Compressed pig parts served in 7.5-inch units

The list just goes on and on. There is an old German saying that goes, "By the time you have eaten all of the wursts of Germany, you will have pig parts coming out the Wazzenschnicter." This certainly proved to be true in our case.

What to Do in Germany

There are a great many spectacularly beautiful villages in Germany, as well as numerous important historic and cultural sites, but you should skip all these because the thing to do is drive really fast. They have these roads in Germany called "autobahns" (meaning, literally, "bahns of the auto") where you can go as fast as you want because there is *no speed limit*. Really! You can get out there and drive like an amphetamine-crazed maniac, and the police will do nothing! And if you don't have a car, you can just steal one, because *car theft is also legal* on the autobahn! So are vagrancy, tax evasion, mail fraud, gambling, narcotics trafficking, and full-body massage! You are going to *love* the autobahn.

```
┌─────────────────────────────────────────────┐
│  🚶🚶  GERMANY FACTS AT A GLANCE              │
│                                               │
│     Unit of Currency: The Doppler            │
│     Barometer: Falling                        │
│     Motto: Vie Guessen Der Caninen Nicht     │
│        Chompen                                │
│        ("These Dogs Probably Will Not Bite You") │
│                                               │
└─────────────────────────────────────────────┘
```

Greece

Greece is where we get a large amount of our Western culture. For example, Zorba the Greek came from there. So did democracy, which is made up of two Greek words, "demo," meaning "people," and "cracy," meaning "wearing stupid hats." The Greeks also gave us the Pythagorean theorem, although after we graduated from high school we gave it back.

Getting to Greece

This is a necessary first step.

Attractions to See in Greece

The biggest city that we have heard of in Greece is **Athens.** According to ancient myth, Athens was created when **Poseidon**, the God of Adventure, struck the ground with his trident, which upset **Ramona**, the Goddess of Humidity and Ranch Dressing, who told **Dagmar**, the God of Variable-Rate Mortgages, who got so mad that he punched

Raoul, the God of Those Little Colored Things You Sprinkle on Cupcakes, and as a result Athens was formed. Of course we now realize that this is **stupid.** Nevertheless many **important old monuments** remain from this period, including the **Metropolis**, the **Pentathlon, Monticello**, the **Telethon**, and the **Tomb of Reebok.** All of these contain a great deal of **very important architecture** that you are welcome to chip off little pieces of for Show and Tell. Outside of Athens is another popular area known to locals as **the rest of Greece.**

 **GREECE FACTS AT A GLANCE**

Unit of Currency: The Sheep
Form of Government: Vague
Liquor Bottles with Worms Inside: Yes

Holland

Holland, also known as "The Hinterlands" or "Sweden," is a plucky nation that has created large sectors of new land by pushing back the sea with a sophisticated complex of dikes that have held up extremely well so far thanks to the vigilance of the Dutch people, as dramatized by the story of the Little Dutch Boy. Remember him? He was walking along one day many years ago when he saw a small leak in one of the dikes, so he plugged the hole with his finger, thereby saving the entire nation. Talk about pluck! Of course he's an old man now, and he has taken to telling passersby that one of these days he's going to pull his finger back out of the goddamn dike and the hell with everybody, but this is no reason for you, as a visitor, to be alarmed, because as a safety precaution, every item of furniture in Holland is legally required to also be usable as a flotation device. Your smart tourist never goes anywhere in the country without carrying, at minimum, a dinette table.

What to See in Holland

The largest city in Holland is **Amsterdam**, a cultural center that boasts many beautiful **historic churches** that you can later claim you were visiting when you were in fact looking at **live naked sex shows** involving as many as **17 individual humans** and the occasional unit of **livestock**. Also do not miss the **Vincent van Gogh Museum**, where you can play the popular **Whack-an-Ear Game**. Out in the countryside you can see **windmills**, many of which are still used for milling wind, as well as millions and millions and millions of **tulips**, so you'll probably just want to stick with the **live naked sex shows**.

🏃🏃 HOLLAND FACTS AT A GLANCE

Unit of Currency: The Grunder
Unit of Livestock's Stage Name: "Bossy"

Iceland

According to a competing travel guidebook, Iceland offers—this is a direct quote—"boiling mud pools." We're on our way!

🚶🚶 ICELAND FACTS AT A GLANCE

Unit of Currency: The Tusk
Biggest Industry: Jumper Cables
Motto: "Skjaarglt Kjooorsklangelt
    KfvoOOOOO . . ."
("Are There Any Boiling Mud Pools Around
HeEEEEE . . .")

Ireland

Ireland is not a large country. A competing guidebook states that "you could drop its entire area into Lake Superior." We certainly do not wish to start rumors, but sometimes we wonder whether these competing guidebooks are on some kind of narcotics. A quick glance at the map will show you that Ireland is in fact nowhere *near* Lake Superior, which is located in Maine. So if your vacation plans include dropping Ireland into a major body of water, a much better choice, in our opinion, would be the Irish Sea, which is far more conveniently located, although during the peak season we do recommend that you have reservations.

Of course there is more to Ireland than water sports. There is also the Irish people, a warm and

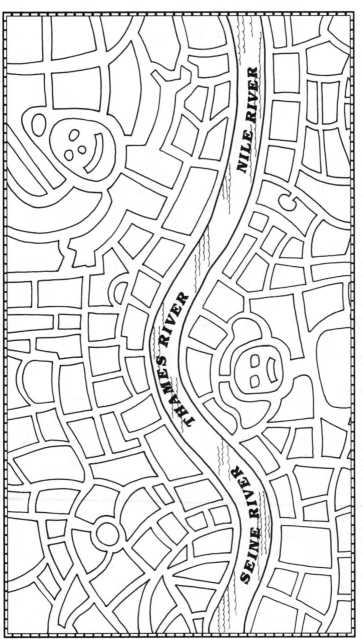

MAP OF DOWNTOWN IRELAND

friendly lot who are constantly saying things like "Begorrah!"[4] Alcohol will do this to people.

The History of Ireland

The history of Ireland dates back a long time to the original inhabitants, the Picts, who were a fun-loving tribe known for their wit. "You sure Pict a winner that time!" is the kind of thing they were always saying, until finally a neighboring tribe called the Celtics got sick and tired of it and came in and, in 432 B.C. on October 8, defeated the Picts in the Battle of Defeating the Picts when John Havlicek sank two free throws in overtime. This led to a long period of time that is virtually incomprehensible if you read about it in the 1966 edition of the *Encyclopaedia Britannica*, which is what we are trying to do, and we are getting a real headache because of sentences like this:

> A well-known territorial unit was the *tricha cet*, corresponding, Giraldus Cambrensis says (*Topographia Hibernica*, iii, 5), to the Welsh *cantref*, 100 households (*villae*).

Ha ha! We bet that Giraldus Cambrensis was one fun dude to hang around with! But anyway, Irish history continued to occur right up to the present time, which is where, according to our calculations, we stand today.

---

[4]Literally, "Your brother Raoul is a fish!"

What to See in Ireland

The main thing to do in Ireland, as Giraldus "Party Animal" Cambrensis states (*Topographia Hibernica*, ivcxxii, section 3, row d, seat 6), is "sit around and drink." But no trip to Ireland is complete without a trip to **Blarney Castle**, where you can kiss the famous **Blarney Stone**, which, according to **ancient legend**, bestows upon each person who kisses it a mild but persistent **mouth fungus**.

 **IRELAND FACTS AT A GLANCE**

Unit of Currency: The Whelk
Households Per Tricha Cet: 100
Shave and a Haircut: Two Bits

Italy

We are definitely talking about a warm and friendly nation here. This nation is so friendly that the leading cause of injury is getting passionately embraced by strangers. One time we were at a restaurant near Rome eating a medium-sized Italian lunch consisting of enough pasta to feed Lithuania for six months, and we happened to mention that the wine tasted good. So the restaurant owner insisted that everybody in our party *had* to go see his wine cellar, which involved climbing down a set of steep rickety stairs into the kind of dark, dank, spider-infested basement that you often see in horror movies, wherein some doomed character goes slowly down the stairs while dramatic music plays in the background and the theater audience is shouting, "DON'T GO DOWN THERE, YOU FOOL!" because they know there's a lunatic lurking in the darkness with a machete and an industrial staple gun. This basement was like that, only it was occupied by something even more dangerous than a homicidal maniac, namely, numerous barrels of wine, which the restaurant owner insisted that we had to drink many samples from, and quite frankly we wonder how we got out of there. In fact some members of our party may still be down there with the spiders, and we urge you to stop in and see them (the spiders) during normal visiting hours.

Speaking of normal visiting hours, Italy doesn't have any, as far as we can tell. Nothing is ever open when it's supposed to be open or closed when it's supposed to be closed, nor does it cost what it's supposed to cost. Also, the buses never seem to go where they're supposed to go. We realize we're making a sweeping generalization here, but as Giraldus Cambrensis so eloquently put it in *Topographia Hibernica*, "tough shit." Nevertheless we urge you to spend some time in this country, although as a precautionary measure you should lose a couple of hundred pounds first.

What to See in Italy

The major city is of course **Rome**, which got its name from the fact that the **Romans** used to live there before the Fall of the Roman Empire. Their **mother** warned them that this would happen. "If you leave your empire there, it's going to fall!" she said, but unfortunately they did not understand English.

Nevertheless, the Romans built many **large broken objects** that you should definitely see, such as the **Renaissance**, the **Piles of Seemingly Random Dirty Stones**, and the **Colosseum**, which was the site of **Super Bowl I**. You must also visit **Vatican City**, where you may see the famous **Sistine Chapel**, which the famous **Anthony L. "Michael" Angelo** had to paint—Believe It or Not!—while *lying on his back*, because due to a **contractor error** the Sistine Chapel is only 18 inches high, so **comfortable clothes** are recommended. The Vatican is also the home of the **Pope**, who, if you pound very hard on his door, will be happy to come out and entertain the kids by twisting balloons into **hilarious animal shapes**. Elsewhere in Italy is the lovely city of **Venice**, which each year attracts **millions of visitors** despite the fact that it is basically an **enormous open sewer**; and **Florence**, home of one of Michael Angelo's most famous works, the **Leaning Tower of Pisa**. Southern Italy is the site of the incredible village of **Pompeii**, which nearly 2,000 years ago was buried under **tons of volcanic ash** and is therefore **invisible**. We don't know why we even brought it **up**.

🚶🚶 ITALY FACTS AT A GLANCE

Unit of Currency: The Lira
(1,000,000,000,000,000 lire = Nothing)
Unit of Time: "A Few Minutes" (A Few
Minutes = Two Days)
Hand Gestures: Permitted

Liechtenstein and Luxembourg

To the best of our knowledge these are not European nations. These are minor characters in William Shakespeare's famous play *Hamlet II: The Next Day*, featuring the famous "shower scene" wherein the immortal bard displays his rollicking wit at its best:

> LIECHTENSTEIN: What, dost thine flaxon augur vepnel sound?
> Nor capsuled repwell florgin haren't ground!
> LUXEMBOURG: Ha ha!

Norway

See "Denmark."

Poland

Poland has experienced a tremendous amount of history due to the fact that it has no natural defensible borders, which makes it very easy to conquer. Many times the other nations didn't even mean to invade Poland; one night they'd simply forget to set the parking brakes on their tanks, and they'd wake up the next morning to discover that, whoosh, they had conquered Poland.

But thanks to advances in international law such as the speed bump, Poland is now a totally independent nation, and it has managed to greatly improve its lifestyle thanks to the introduction of modern Western conveniences such as food. Today Poland proudly boasts the nickname "The North Dakota of Europe," and is well worth a visit if you happen to be in the neighborhood for some reason, such as your plane has crashed.

What to See in Poland

They have some really sharp **tractors**.

POLAND FACTS AT A GLANCE

Unit of Currency: The Grzbwczwcz
Population: 30 million
Light-Bulb-Changing Capability: 10 million

Portugal

Portugal is a small but, we are sure, proud nation located somewhere in Europe and boasting a history. During the Age of Exploration, Portugal produced many great navigators, men such as Vasco da Gama (literally, "Vasco the Gama"), who set out across the vast, stormy Atlantic Ocean in tiny ships, which of course immediately sank like stones, thus paving the way for the Age of Remaining on Land. Today the main industry in Portugal is manufacturing the famous Portuguese man-of-war, which is a type of jellyfish that can sting you to death if provoked, so tipping is strongly recommended.

PORTUGAL FACTS AT A GLANCE

Unit of Currency: The Arriba
Language: None

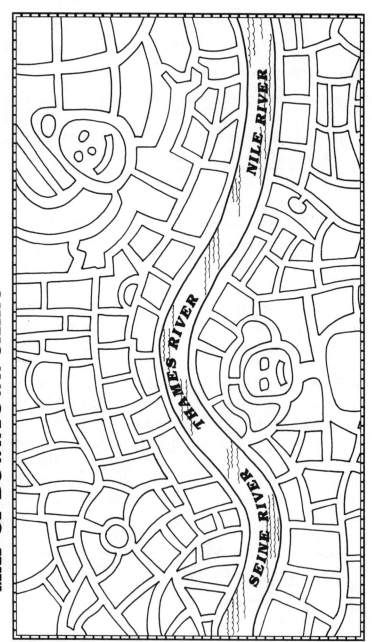

MAP OF DOWNTOWN CAIRO

Spain

At one time Spain was one of the world's great powers, although under the leadership of General Francisco Franco (1578–1983) the nation gradually declined into total insignificance. There is no need, however, for you to rub this in. Be gracious, is our advice. For example, in a restaurant you might exclaim: "This food is certainly delicious! Especially considering that Spain is now a fourth-rate power!" Your hosts are sure to appreciate your thoughtfulness, and may even insist that you join in one of Spain's most glorious traditions: Getting Run Over by Bulls. This extremely exciting event, wherein live irate bulls are set loose in public streets, was originally held during the Festival of St. Raoul of the Fishes (October 8), but it has become so popular that in heavily touristed areas the bulls are released several times a day, sometimes in hotel lobbies. Wear comfortable shoes.

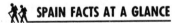 **SPAIN FACTS AT A GLANCE**

Unit of Currency: The Caramba
Closed: Weekdays

Sweden

See "Norway."

Switzerland

When we think of Switzerland, the picturesque image that springs into our minds is that of men standing on top of Alps wearing comical shorts and making sounds that can only result from a major hormonal imbalance. But Switzerland is also famous for its tidiness. It makes some of the other tidy nations, such as Germany and Austria, look like giant septic tanks. Switzerland has an extremely strict Neatness Code. If you appear in public with your hair mussed up, or armpit stains on your shirt, the famous Swiss Neatness Police will suck you up with a giant vacuum cleaner and put you in a jail cell infested with sanitary laboratory rats. You would probably rot in there, but Switzerland doesn't even permit *bacteria*.

What to Do in Switzerland

You should open a **Swiss bank account**, because (a) you get a **toaster** and (b) you never have to pay **income taxes** again. The Internal Revenue Service has no jurisdiction in Switzerland. When you fill out your tax return, you just write, "**Ha ha,** I have a Swiss bank account and just TRY TO GET IT, YOU **SUCKERS**!" and all the IRS can do is gnash its **teeth**. You can trust us when we tell you this. We're a **guidebook**.

🚶🚶 SWITZERLAND FACTS AT A GLANCE

Unit of Currency: The Cubit
This Chapter Is Finally: Finished
Time for a: Beer

Staying in Hotels

(OR: WE'RE VERY SORRY, BUT YOUR CHAPTER IS NOT READY YET)

Your hotel is your "home away from home," and as such you expect it to provide you with the comforts and conveniences you have in your own dwelling, such as privacy, security, a warm bed, a clean bathroom, a hot shower, Anthony Perkins standing just outside the shower curtain holding a knife the size of New Jersey, etc.

Of course we are just pulling your leg. Despite the widespread recurring nightmares created by the movie *Psycho*, the truth is that, of the millions of guests who stay in the nation's hotels each year, only about 3 percent are ever actually stabbed to death while in the shower.[1] A far higher percentage are

---

[1] Source: The American Automobile Association

stabbed to death while talking really loud in the halls at 2:30 in the morning. If you've ever stayed at a hotel, you have heard these people. They stagger up from the bar, then they stand directly outside your room and, in booming voices, have conversations like this:

FIRST LOUD PERSON: Well, it's about time to turn in!

SECOND LOUD PERSON: I guess so! What time is it?

FIRST LOUD PERSON: Whoa! It's 2:30 A.M.!

SECOND LOUD PERSON: Whoa! It's time to turn in!

FIRST LOUD PERSON: I'll say it is!

SECOND LOUD PERSON: Two-thirty A.M.!

FIRST LOUD PERSON: Whoa!

SECOND LOUD PERSON: It's definitely time to turn in!

FIRST LOUD PERSON: I'll say it is!

SECOND LOUD PERSON: You can say that agAAAAAAIEEEEEE (*sound of both loud persons being stabbed to death by pajama-clad hotel guests who have lunged out into the hallway wielding shrimp-cocktail forks obtained earlier from Room Service*)

There is no need to concern yourself about this. At your better hotels, the bodies will be picked up within hours. Other signs that you are in a quality hotel include the following:

1. *You can never be sure which floor the lobby is on.* A quality hotel will have about six Mystery Floors where the lobby should be,

identified on the elevator buttons only by code letters such as G, P, M, LL, and Ph.D. Guests from hotel-deprived regions such as Mississippi will sometimes become disoriented and ride the elevator for days, surviving on complimentary pillow mints donated by other guests.

2. *You have to tip roughly a dozen men just to check in.* The instant you arrive at a quality hotel, at least two friendly men dressed in nicer outfits than you wore at your first wedding will bustle up, open the car door for you, and say: "Welcome to the Hyatt Sheraton Hilton Crowne Royale Majestic Princess! Let us assist you with your luggage!" Even if the airline lost your luggage and your total possessions consist of a package of Tums, these men will snatch it away from you and assist you with it. The instant you tip them, they will hand your luggage to other uniformed men, who will pass it along to still *other* men, until you are being assisted by roughly one uniformed man for each actual Tum.

3. *The bellperson will not leave you alone in your room until he has given you a briefing lasting at least as long as your sophomore year in high school.* This will include such helpful information as:
   • Where the bathroom is.
   • Where the windows are.
   • Where the bed is.
   • Where to find the complimentary bathrobe

that you are welcome to take with you, in which case they will be happy to add a charge of $298 to your bill.

- Where the bathroom is again, in case you forgot.
- How you operate the television.[2]
- What the bellperson's name is[3] in case you need anything.[4]

The only thing the bellperson will leave out is the part about how you will have to get up at 2:30 A.M. to kill the loud hallway talkers, but this is because he doesn't want to spoil the surprise.

4. *There will be a choice of six in-room movies,[5] all of which you have already seen except for the dirty one.* However, we do not recommend that you watch the dirty movie, because it will go on your hotel bill, which could cause embarrassment when you check out the next morning and the desk clerk, in a hearty voice that echoes all over the lobby, says: "We certainly hope you enjoyed your stay at the Hyatt Sheraton Hilton Crowne Royale Majestic Princess, Mr. Penderson, especially your in-room viewing of *Big Hooter Mommas*."

Also every hotel, no matter what level of quality, is required by state law to have a little framed document in every room with the following notification:

---

[2]By turning it on
[3]Bob.
[4]Such as you feel a sudden urge to give somebody a tip.
[5]Including *The Bad News Bears*.

NOTIFICATION

In accordance with **sec. 3.409583 par. 2343.4**, be advised that the operator of this hotel is not **responsible** for any **loss, theft** or **damage** to any **jewelry, money or other valuables** that you may sustain because of **carelessness, burglars,** or **anybody else** sneaking into your hotel room in the **dead of night** armed with **guns, knives, cattle prods, deadly poison black mamba snakes** or **whatever** you better just give them **whatever they want** because the owner is not going to get **involved** even if they **tie you to the bed** with **the belt from your complimentary bathrobe** and torture **you** by pouring your **complimentary hair conditioner** into your **eyes** you can go ahead and **scream all you want** because in accordance with **sec. 3.409583 par. 2343.4,** be advised that ha ha the **operator** of this hotel does not have to do **shit.**

STAYING AT QUAINT LITTLE COUNTRY INNS

Of course sometimes you get sick and tired of staying in big, modern hotels, where all you are is an impersonal room number, and nobody ever talks to you, and you never have to share a bathroom with total strangers. For a change of pace from this kind of stifling uniformity, you want to stay at a quaint little country inn.

The best kind of quaint country inn is the kind that's owned and operated by a couple named Dick and Marge who've been married for roughly 158 years and are bored to death with each other and consequently are thrilled that you have come out into the country to give them somebody to talk to and eavesdrop on and study the personal habits of.

"Don't mind me!" Marge will say eight or nine

times just during breakfast, which you eat at a table located approximately four feet from where she is working in the kitchen. "I know you two are here for a romantic weekend, and I don't want you to even notice I'm here! Although Dick did want me to ask you to please not flush any more condoms down the toilet like you did twice last night, because sometimes they mess up the septic system. We had one couple from New Jersey, the Floogermans, and they were using the Trojan lubricated condom with the reservoir tip, and they flushed *four* of them on one night, let me see"—she consults her records—"it was the night of June 12, 1987, and next day we had raw sewage in the azaleas, and Dick—Dick loves those azaleas—he had a fit. He even—get this—he even got out his old machete and sharpened it up. I said, 'Dick, what are you gonna do? Chop off their heads just because they flushed some condoms down the toilet?' Ha ha! I had to give him one of those shots to calm him down, and he still carries a little piece of paper in his wallet with the Floogermans' home address. He LOVES those azaleas. But listen to me chattering on! You just never mind me over here. Do you want some more waffles? I didn't even realize you could *have* waffles, if you were diabetic, which I'm assuming you are from those pills in your toiletries case with your Valium. Lately I just can't seem to get Dick to take his medication, and I really wish he would because he's started talking to his snakes again. I wish we didn't even have those things in the house, after what happened to those people from Ohio, the Fweemers. Although I understand that a lot of the time those paralysis things are temporary.

But listen to me! Here I am talking a mile a minute, and you two lovebirds are trying to have a quiet breakfast alone! I do tend to rattle on so, and sometimes Dick—I'm sure he's just kidding—sometimes Dick says if I don't shut up, he's gonna put me down in the basement, with those things he ordered from *Soldier of Fortune* magazine. Don't go down there, whatever you do. But you just make yourselves totally at home here, and enjoy your time together, and do whatever you want and just forget that we're even here. By the way, that light fixture over your bed is just a light fixture. It is *not* a camera. Here comes Dick now! What's the matter, honey?''

Camping:

NATURE'S WAY OF PROMOTING THE MOTEL INDUSTRY

So far we've discussed many exciting travel destinations, but all of them lack an element that is too often missing from the stressful, high-pressure urban environment most of us live in. That element is: dirt. Also missing from the urban environment are snakes, pit toilets, and tiny black flies that crawl up your nose. To experience these things, you need to locate some Nature and go camping in it.

WHERE NATURE IS LOCATED

Nature is located mainly in national parks, which are vast tracts of wilderness that have been set aside by the United States government so citizens will always have someplace to go where they can be attacked by bears. And we're not talking about ordinary civilian bears, either: We're talking about *federal* bears, which can behave however they want to because they are protected by the same union as postal clerks.

You also want to be on the lookout for federal moose. I had a moose encounter once, when my wife and I were camping in Yellowstone National Park, which is popular with nature lovers because it has dangerous geysers of superheated steam that come shooting up out of the ground, exactly like in New York City, except that the Yellowstone geysers operate on a schedule. Anyway, one morning I woke up and went outside to savor the dawn's ever-changing subtle beauty, by which I mean take a leak, and there, maybe fifteen feet away, was an animal approximately the size of the Western Hemisphere and shaped like a horse with a severe steroid problem. It pretended to be peacefully eating moss, but this was clearly a clever ruse designed to lull me into believing that it was a gentle, moss-eating creature. Obviously no creature gets to be that large by eating moss. A creature gets to be that large by stomping other creatures to death with its giant hooves. Clearly what it wanted me to do was approach it, so it could convert me into a wilderness pizza while bellowing triumphant moss-breath bellows into the morning air. Fortunately I am an experienced woodsperson, so I had the presence of mind to follow the Recommended Wilderness Moose-Encounter Procedure, which was to get in the car and indicate to my wife, via a system of coded horn-honks, that she was to pack up all our equipment and put it in the car trunk, and then get in the trunk herself, so that I would not have to open the actual door until we had relocated to a safer area, such as Ohio.

This chilling story is yet another reminder of the importance of:

SELECTING THE PROPER CAMPSITE

Selecting the proper campsite can mean the difference between survival and death in the wilderness, so you, the woodsperson, must always scrutinize the terrain carefully to make sure that it can provide you with the basic necessities, the main one being a metal thing that sticks out of the ground where you hook up the air conditioner on your recreational vehicle. I'm assuming here that you have a recreational vehicle, which has been the preferred mode of camping in America ever since the early pioneers traveled westward in primitive, oxen-drawn Winnebagos.

Of course there are some thoughtful, environmentally sensitive ecology nuts who prefer to camp in tents, which are fine except for four things:

1. All tent-erection instructions are written by the Internal Revenue Service ("Insert ferrule

post into whippet grommet, or 23 percent of your gross deductible adjustables, whichever is more difficult'').

2. It always rains on tents. Rainstorms will travel thousands of miles against the prevailing winds for the opportunity to rain on a tent, which is bad because:

3. Tents contain mildews, which are tiny one-celled animals that are activated by moisture and immediately start committing one-celled acts of flatulence, so that before long it smells like you're sleeping in a giant unwashed gym sock.

4. Tents are highly attractive to bears. When bears are young, their parents give them, as a treat, little camper-shaped candies in little tent wrappers.

So I'm recommending a major recreational vehicle, the kind that has a VCR-equipped recreation room and consumes the annual energy output of Syria merely to operate the windshield wipers. Other wilderness survival equipment that you should always take along includes:

- A hatchet, in case you need to fix the VCR
- Cheez-Its
- A flashlight last used in 1973, with what appears to be penicillin mold growing on the batteries

And speaking of penicillin, you need to know:

WHAT TO DO IN A WILDERNESS MEDICAL EMERGENCY

Experts agree that the most important rule in a wilderness medical emergency is: *Keep your head down on the follow-through.* No! My mistake! That's the most important rule in *golf.* The most important rule in a wilderness medical emergency is: *Don't panic.* To prevent the victim from going into shock, you must reassure him, as calmly as possible, that everything's going to be fine:

> VICTIM *(clearly frightened)*: Am I going to be okay?
>
> YOU *(in a soothing voice)*: Of course you are! I'm sure we'll find your legs around here someplace!
>
> VICTIM *(relieved)*: Whew! You got any Cheez-Its?

Once the victim has been calmed, you need to obtain pertinent information by asking the following Standard Medical Questions:

1. Does he have medical insurance?
2. Does his spouse have medical insurance?
3. Was he referred to this wilderness by another doctor?
4. How much does he weigh?
5. Does that figure include legs?

Write this information down on a medical chart, then give the victim a 1986 copy of *Fortune* magazine to read while you decide on the correct course of treatment. This will depend on the exact nature of the injury. For example, if it's mushroom poisoning or a broken limb, you'll need to apply a tourniquet. Whereas if it's a snake bite, then you need to determine whether the snake was poisonous, which will be indicated by tiny markings on the snake's stomach as follows:

WARNING! POISON SNAKE!

ACHTUNG! SCHLANGE SCHNAPPENKILLEN!

In this case, you need to apply a tourniquet to the snake, as shown in Figure 1.

FUN FAMILY WILDERNESS ACTIVITIES

There are so many fun things for a family to do together in the wilderness that I hardly know where to start. One proven barrel of wilderness laughs is to try to identify specific kinds of trees by looking at the bark, leaves, federal identification plaques, etc. This activity is bound to provide many seconds of enjoyment for the youngsters. ("This one's an oak!" "No it's not!" "You suck!") Later on, you can play Survival Adventure, where the children, using only a compass and a map, must try to figure out what city Mom and Dad have driven to.

But the greatest camping fun comes at night, when everybody gathers 'round the campfire and sings campfire songs. Some of our "old family favorites" include:

FIGURE 1. PUTTING A TOURNIQUET ON A SNAKE

1. HAVE SNAKE LIE DOWN.

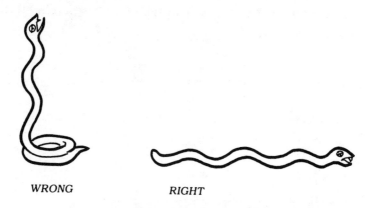

WRONG   *RIGHT*

2. APPLY TOURNIQUET TO SNAKE'S BODY.

WRONG

RIGHT

Source: The Red Cross

I've Been Workin' on the Railroad

Oh, I've been workin' on the railroad,
With a banjo on my knee.
We will kill the old red rooster
We will kill the old red rooster
We will kill the old red rooster
And you better not get in our way.

Michael Row the Boat Ashore

Michael row the boat ashore, Alleluia!
Michael row the boat ashore, Alleluia!
Michael row the damn boat ashore, Alleluia!
Lenore threw up in the tackle box.

Camptown Races

Camptown ladies sing this song: Doo-dah, doo-dah
Camptown ladies been off their medication
And they are none too fond of the old red rooster,
    either.

After the singing, it's time for Dad to prepare the children for bedtime by telling them a traditional campfire story. To qualify as traditional, the story has to adhere to the following guidelines, established by the National Park Service:

1. It has to begin Many Years Ago when some people camped Right in This Very Forest on a night Exactly Like Tonight.
2. People warned them not to camp here, but they paid no attention.
3. People said, "I wouldn't go back in there if I were you! That's the lair of the [select one]:

a. Snake Man!''
b. Swamp Devil!''
c. Giant Radioactive Meat-Eating Box Turtle of Death!''
4. But the campers just laughed.
5. "Ha ha!'' were their exact words.
6. Until they found little Jennifer's gallbladder on the Hibachi.

And so on. Dad should tell this story in a soft, almost hypnotic voice, lulling the children into a trance-like state in which they are aware of nothing except the story and the terror and the still, sinister darkness all around them and

OHMIGOD HERE IT COMES

And then it's time for everybody to "call it a night'' and climb, all five of you, into the sleeping bag with Mom.

WELCOME HOME!

OR: ''THAT'S ODD! OUR HOUSE *USED* TO BE RIGHT HERE!''

As we have seen in the preceding chapters, traveling is a tremendous amount of fun, but eventually[1] you become too tired and broke and diseased to continue. Then it's time to come home, drop your suitcases right at the front door, kick off your shoes, and stagger into the kitchen to quench your thirst with a nice cold . . . **NO**

DON'T OPEN THE
REFRIGERATOR AIEEEEEE . . .

You have *no idea* what kinds of fierce predatory meat-eating fungi have been growing in there while

[1]Sometimes in less than an hour

you were gone. They've been feeding on the highly nutritious Chinese take-out food that you've been wisely storing in the back of your refrigerator for several months in case it suddenly appreciates in value. Your refrigerator has developed individual mold spores the size of Doberman pinschers, and they are going to be *very angry* if you just barge into their territory and try to grab something. The American Medical Association, in an alarming 1989 report,[2] stated that the leading cause of death among Americans returning from trips is being attacked by refrigerator mold. "Never enter your kitchen after a trip without a working flamethrower in your hand," advises the AMA.

This is assuming, of course, that you still *have* a kitchen. There's always the possibility that your house has burned down, and the only thing that survived the fire is the stack of credit-card bills documenting all the shrewd purchases you made on your trip, such as the $197.50 Authentic Souvenir Limbo Stick that was confiscated by U.S. Customs because it contained lethal parasites.

And even if your house is still there, there's always the chance that your plumbing—which has sophisticated electronic sensors so it knows the instant you leave home—has developed a leak, which doesn't sound like such a big deal until you consider that the Grand Canyon, for example, is basically the result of water damage.

And speaking of damages, you should check the dense growth that has sprung up around your house

[2]There is no further information contained in this footnote

in case it contains the moaning, semi-deceased body of a mailperson or door-to-door salesperson, or meter reader, or one of the dozens of other people who could have visited your house while you were gone and tripped on a Dangerous Hazard in your yard, such as the ground, causing him to fall and severely injure his back, resulting in so much Pain and Suffering that he has been unable to move, except of course to notify his attorney and put a down payment on a motor yacht the size of Utica, New York.

But never mind these temporary problems. The point is that you had *fun*, right? Remember the Old Traveler's Saying: "You may lose your money and your health and your sanity and some important organs, but they can't take away your travel memories unless they hit you hard on the head." These are the words I live by, as a traveler, and in these pages I've tried to share my vast knowledge with you as a way of saying "Thank You!" for buying this book.

Unless of course you just borrowed this book, in which case I hope that the next time you travel, your luggage winds up on a space probe.